Bicycling Guide to the Mississippi River Trail

FOREWORD

Welcome to the inaugural Bicycling Guide to the Mississippi River Trail! Authored by Bob Robinson, an avid cyclist from Fort Smith, Arkansas, the book offers a host of riding adventures, short and long, through some of the most unique and culturally significant areas in America.

Staff and board alike at Mississippi River Trail, Inc. applaud Bob's grueling research efforts that led to a publication with thorough trip planning details for each segment of the corridor. The narrative offers you, the reader, a bird's eye view of each section. Camping, lodging, and bike shop information, including addresses and phone numbers, makes it easy to plan your adventure with confidence.

By exploring the corridor myself, I have gained a wealth of information, experienced delights beyond imagination, met like-minded folks in great numbers, and brought home a wealth of happy memories that will last a lifetime. From the secret mysteries of the Ojibwa Indians at Lake Itasca, Minnesota, to the Cajun folklore and New Orleans jazz, the Mississippi River Trail takes you deep into the history of the Mississippi River. Explore picturesque shipping and commerce towns rife with the ways of old, experience urban culture and nightlife in some of America's most important cities, and shake hands with small town folks eager to greet you at every stop.

This book, a goal of Mississippi River Trail, Inc. since its inception in 1996, will open up a new world of cycling opportunities for residents and visitors alike. So, join us on the Mississippi River journey as we work to promote tourism opportunities for cyclists along the nation's second longest, and the world's fourth longest, river!

Happy cycling!

Terry Eastin
Executive Director, Mississippi River Trail, Inc.

Bicycling Guide to the Mississippi River Trail

Published by
Spirits Creek
Fort Smith, Arkansas

Copyright © 2008 by Bob Robinson

Edited by Dawna Stultz Robinson and Linda Mills Boyd
Cover and Page Layout by Laura Wattles
All photographs by Bob Robinson and Dawna Robinson, with the
exception of the cover photo.

Cover photo and retouching courtesy of David Larson – Minnesota
Department of Transportation. *Bicyclists enjoying the Grand Rounds Scenic
Byway along the Mississippi River in Minneapolis, Minnesota. This is also
designated as the Great River Road Scenic Byway.*

Library of Congress Control Number: 2008906698

ISBN 978-0-9818952-0-8

Contents

Tennessee

Arkansas

Mississippi

Louisiana

This book is dedicated to Dawna Robinson—my best friend, my partner for life, my sweetheart, who is also my wife. Thank you for all of your support.

Acknowledgments:

I would like to express my appreciation to the following people who contributed to this book: Dawna Robinson, Laura Wattles, Linda Mills Boyd, Terry Eastin, Ken Eastin, Carol Zoff, Michelle Natrop, Cindy Habedank, Thomas Huber, Michael Rewey, Tiffani Jackson, John Frusha, Dan Jatres, Tim Ernst, Terry Whaley, Scott Chapman, Todd Antoine, Mark Ackelsone, Andrea Chase, Jim Gonyier, Caryn Giarratono, Jim Keyoth, Ed Barsotti, Mark Wyatt, David Larson, Munnie Jordan, Dorian Grilley, Briggs Hopson, and everyone who works for the Department of Transportation, and the Department of Natural Resources in each state that the route passes through. I could not have written the book without them. I also would like to recognize the League of Illinois Bicyclists and the Iowa Bicycle Coalition for their work in establishing and promoting the Mississippi River Trail in their states.

Thank you all.

Introduction

The Mississippi River Trail is America's newest cross-country bicycle route. The course follows the Mississippi River corridor from its headwaters at Itasca State Park in Minnesota, to the southernmost point in Louisiana, on the Gulf of Mexico. The route consists of over 3,000 miles of roads and bike/pedestrian pathways that pass through 10 states. When possible, the MRT follows rural roads that keep cyclists in close contact with the river, as it transitions from a small pristine stream to the country's largest shipping waterway.

As the MRT follows the Mississippi River through the nation's heartland, it takes cyclists past countless scenic views and a number of historic monuments. One of the main features that draw cyclists to the MRT is the availability of services along the route, no matter what their daily mileage may be. Many of the quaint picturesque communities along the route have long been popular destinations for travelers, and are well equipped to accommodate their needs. The MRT passes a number of state parks and recreation areas that offer campgrounds and interpretive displays on the interesting history of the area. Many of the states that border the Mississippi River have their own MRT routes, providing opportunities for enjoyable loop tours. Also, with the route's central location, many of the lower-48 states are within a day's drive to a section of the MRT.

Using This Guide

This guide is not a personal journal of my adventures while riding the MRT. Rather, it is a collection of relevant materials for cyclists to use to create their own adventures. My intention was to create a guidebook that would include all necessary information that cyclists need to plan and to ride the MRT, and still limit the book to a manageable size that would be convenient for cyclists to carry with them.

In this guidebook, each state is divided into sections. The mileage for each section is not based on the number of miles cyclists should ride each day. Not all cyclists share the same agenda. Instead, each section provides the materials each cyclist needs to create their own daily schedule, and the flexibility to adjust their schedule as needed. Each section includes text, services, a map, and the all-important Mileage Log. When using this material, I suggest that you first read the text associated with a section, to familiarize yourself with the route, and any attractions to visit along the ride. The services included will help you select a target destination for the day's ride, and the map provides an overall understanding of the route. Be sure to read the Mileage Log to familiarize yourself with the turns involved in the first part of your ride, and keep it handy as a reference during your ride.

Text

The text provides a running account of the route through the associated section, and points out many of its attractions. It relates the history of the area, so that cyclists can better appreciate the communities and scenery along the route. The text also serves to complement the Mileage Log, by providing greater detail for complicated directions or other potential hazards.

Acronyms commonly used within the text are MRT (Mississippi River Trail), MR (Mississippi River), and RS (Recommended Stop). The guidebook does not identify every attraction that the MRT passes as a RS. RS is generally a stop that cyclists might pass unnoticed, or may not otherwise take the time to investigate, but is an attraction they might find interesting or enjoyable to visit.

Services

Where services are available, each section in the guide lists camping, lodging, and bike shops. For large cities, all available lodging establishments may not be listed. Those services that are preceded by an asterisk (*) are located immediately along the route.

Mileage Log

Column headings:

Miles N/S: Accumulated miles for the referenced section, when riding from north to south.

Directions: Instructions and points of interest along the route. Rows beginning with an * are intended as an FYI, such as a town or a turn for an optional side trip.

Dist: The distance in miles to travel for the associated instruction.

S: The width of a paved shoulder in feet.

T: Rating for traffic using a scale of Low, Medium, or Heavy.

Services: C= camping, G = a full grocery store, L = lodging, such as a motel, bed-and-breakfast, lodge, etc., Q = a type of business where cyclists can stop for a quick snack, such as a convenience store, small grocery, etc. R = a restaurant that serves prepared foods. Available services will be listed both for the section of

road that they are on, and the town they are located in.
Miles S/N: Reversed accumulated miles for the referenced section, for cyclists traveling south to north.

Acronyms used in the Mileage Log directions:
CR: County Road, L: Left, R: Right, SH: State Highway, SL: Stop Light, SS: Stop Sign, YS: Yield Sign.

Map:

MAP KEY

————	MRT Route	☐	County road
————	Non-MRT highway	○	State highway
⬠	US highway	▲	Camping
⬠	Interstate highway	☐	Monument

Equipment

If you have a bike, you can tour. My first tour was on a 10-speed Huffy® with a daypack strapped to a bolt-on rack. I do admit that touring is a lot more enjoyable with my Fuji® Touring bike and Jandd® Large Mountain Panniers. However, the equipment required depends on the type of touring you will be doing. For those who plan to ride non-supported across the entire MRT, or riding it in large segments, I suggest that you read a book on bicycle touring. Contact Adventure Cycling Association for a list of available publications. For those cyclists who plan to ride the MRT supported, a small bag to carry snacks, tools, and extra clothing may be all you need. I met a pair of cyclists on the route who plan to ride the entire MRT in segments, over extended weekends. All they plan to carry with them is the equipment they carry on a normal day-ride.

If you are touring unsupported, I do recommend that you carry extra food. There is always a chance that a listed service might be closed when you need it. As a rule when touring unsupported, I carry a small plastic jar of peanut butter, a few tortillas, and a package of ramen noodles.

Safety

The list of the roads described in this guidebook as the designated route of the Mississippi River Trail, is not an indication that they are safe for cyclists. When you ride the roads described in this book, you assume responsibility for your own safety. Most of the route of the Mississippi River Trail follows highways that are used by motor vehicles, and dangers that are normally associated with riding such roads exist while riding the Mississippi River Trail.

Weather: Average High/Low/Rainfall

City, State	Jan Hi Lo Rn	Feb Hi Lo Rn	Mar Hi Lo Rn	Apr Hi Lo Rn	May Hi Lo Rn	Jun Hi Lo Rn	Jul Hi Lo Rn	Aug Hi Lo Rn	Sep Hi Lo Rn	Oct Hi Lo Rn	Nov Hi Lo Rn	Dec Hi Lo Rn
Bemidji, MN	16 -4 .69	24 3 .57	36 16 .86	53 30 1.52	67 43 2.62	75 52 4.09	79 57 4.33	77 55 3.50	66 45 2.75	54 35 2.26	34 19 1.12	21 3 .63
St. Paul, MN	23 6 1.02	30 13 .78	42 24 1.92	58 36 2.54	71 48 3.73	79 58 4.98	83 63 4.41	81 61 4.37	72 52 3.20	59 40 2.51	41 26 2.09	27 12 1.04
Dubuque IA	27 9 1.16	34 15 1.09	45 26 2.13	60 38 3.26	72 50 3.82	82 61 4.27	85 65 4.28	83 63 4.19	74 54 3.61	62 42 2.39	45 29 2.33	32 16 1.43
St Louis, MO	38 21 2.01	45 26 2.06	55 36 3.70	66 47 3.82	77 57 3.92	86 66 3.73	91 71 3.78	88 69 3.70	81 61 2.69	69 49 2.81	54 38 4.06	42 27 2.56
Memphis TN	49 31 4.24	55 36 4.31	63 44 5.58	72 52 5.79	80 61 5.15	89 69 4.30	92 73 4.22	91 71 3.00	85 64 3.31	75 52 3.31	62 43 5.76	52 34 5.68
Helena, AR	49 30 4.60	55 34 4.08	64 43 5.35	74 51 5.36	82 60 5.67	90 68 4.76	93 72 3.74	92 70 2.74	86 63 3.16	76 51 3.69	63 41 5.51	53 33 5.39
New Orleans, LA	62 43 5.87	65 46 5.47	72 53 5.24	78 58 5.02	85 66 4.62	89 72 6.83	91 74 6.20	91 74 6.15	87 71 5.55	80 60 3.05	71 52 5.09	65 46 5.07

MINNESOTA

The Minnesota portion of the MRT shadows the Mississippi River as it cuts through the central heartland region of the state, then angles across to the state's southeastern corner. Riding along county roads, the cyclist views the river as a gentle stream flowing through lake resort areas, rural farmland and wooded forest. The trail routes you past beautiful lush gardens in St. Cloud and through downtown Minneapolis and St. Paul on a separated bike path along the banks of the river. After leaving these major cities behind, the MRT follows several busy highways, returning the cyclist to lesser-traveled county roads when feasible. In the southern portion of the state, the route uses large sections of US 61. This highway has heavy traffic, but maintains a good paved shoulder. For those organizing multi-day touring loops, the following section descriptions include several bridges that connect to the Wisconsin MRT for the return ride.

At the time of this writing, Minnesota's MRT does not have route signs installed; however, the DOT provided me a detailed description of the route and all the latest revisions, right up to when the guide went to press. So cyclists should have no difficulty following the 568 mile route through the state.

Minnesota: Section 1
Itasca State Park to Bena (79 miles)

The MRT adventure begins at Itasca State Park. Itasca is Minnesota's oldest state park and the second-oldest in the United States. If your schedule allows, plan time for exploring the exciting activities this park offers. Be sure to ride the 11-mile Wilderness Drive that circles the park. Along the ride, stop to enjoy the view from atop the restored 100-foot-tall fire tower, hike through the 300-year-old red pine trees of Preacher's Grove, and then finish the loop on the paved bike path. The park includes camping, interpretive exhibits, historical displays, and a lake boat tour. Before beginning your MRT ride, treat yourself to dinner and a room at the 1905 Historic Douglas Lodge.

When you have completed your visit of the park and are ready to begin the MRT, follow the signs to the official headwaters of the Mississippi River. Remove your shoes and wade across the narrow stream that is gently flowing out of Lake Itasca, dip your rear tire in the water, then have your picture taken in front of the monument.

You may be reluctant to do this, with all the tourists watching on, but after the ride is over you'll be glad you performed these traditional rituals because the memories will be priceless.

The author ankle deep in the headwaters of the Mighty Mississippi River.

The Mileage Log officially begins as you exit the Mary Gibbs Mississippi Headwaters parking lot. Your adrenalin will be pumping and you'll be eager to get started, but don't race through these opening miles. Take time to enjoy the scenery. On the 30-plus miles to Bemidji, you'll be riding on quiet county roads bordered by commercial pine forests and classic rural farms with large barns topped by weather vanes. These old barns are full of character, unlike the boxes they build now. In the distance you'll see some of the small lakes that make Minnesota the Land of 10,000 Lakes. In the Mileage Log, I include each MR crossing. Don't worry; I don't do this throughout the entire guide. I thought it was interesting to follow the progress of the tiny stream I waded across as it goes through its transformation into the mighty, mile-wide waterway later on the MRT. As you witness how the MR is linked between so many lakes, you can appreciate why early explorers like Zebulon Pike, Giacomo Beltrami, and Henry Schoolcraft had so much difficulty locating the headwaters of the great river. It wasn't until after following the advice of American Indians that Schoolcraft discovered the true source and named it Lake Itasca, derived from a Latin phrase meaning "true head."

When you reach Bemidji, if you want to claim that you rode across the entire country, border to border, take US 71 north for about 100 miles to touch a bike tire on Canadian soil. However, this is not required to receive your certificate of completion for the MRT.

In Bemidji the MRT routes cyclists past all services except camping. When you reach the Tourist Information Center you can avoid some of the traffic by taking the bike path out of the parking lot. You can't miss the Center; just look for the giant statues of Paul Bunyan and Babe. The bike path will take you to 1st Street, where there is a painted bike lane. If you are ready to camp, and don't mind riding 7.5 miles off the MRT, you can turn left off 1st Street onto Gould Avenue. This will lead to the trailhead of a bike path that will take you to Lake Bemidji State Park campground. This bike path is also the northern end of the Paul Bunyan Trail. If you are interested in a 300-plus-mile loop, you could follow the MRT to the town of Baxter, then return via the PBT. The PBT is a premier 100-plus-mile bicycle path, mainly following the Burlington Northern Railroad grade connecting Baxter and Lake Bemidji State Park. This is a sweet trail, and if you can work it into your schedule you will be glad you did. At the time of this writing, all the trail is paved except a 12-mile stretch from Guthrie to Walker. I include a guide for the PBT in the alternate route section located at the end of the Minnesota chapter. I'm sure this trail is destined for the Rails to Trails Hall of Fame.

After leaving Bemidji, the next large town you pass through is Grand Rapids. However, there are inviting lake resorts and a few convenience stores scattered along the route, especially along CR 91 and CR 9. I've listed several to assist you in planning your trip. If you are camping, be sure to carry backup food in case the convenience stores and restaurants are closed. Also, keep in mind that CR 91/54 passes through the Chippewa National Forest, which allows dispersed camping, meaning you can camp pretty much wherever you want. Exercise safety with campfires, and practice "leave no trace" guidelines. Keep your eyes open for bald eagles as you ride through the Chippewa National Forest. This area has the highest breeding density of bald eagles in the lower 48. It is also home to more than 1,700 timber wolves. When I rode CR 91, there was a raccoon on the highway shoulder. As I reached it, the raccoon took off running down the road in the same direction I was riding. I had the unique experience of riding a hundred feet with a raccoon at my side. The wildlife, forests, swampland, lakes, and low traffic make it a really nice environment for riding a bike.

Looking at the map, you've probably been thinking there have been a lot of different highway numbers. I don't know the history of this, but Minnesota changes the highway numbers for county roads each time it crosses a county line. It's not a problem. In the Mileage Log, if there is no turn involved, I list the combination of road numbers on the same line, separating them with a slash. This is also helpful for cyclists riding south to north—to know the highway number posted at the opposite end of a highway.

When you first turn on to US 2, you'll pass a roadside oddity, the Big Fish Supper Club. There is nothing unusual about the restaurant itself. It wasn't even open the last time I rode through. The shape of the restaurant as a 65-foot-long concrete muskie is what makes this a landmark. At one point there was a hamburger stand in the fish, but now it's only a place to stop and have your picture taken standing in the fish's mouth. Since this is right on the road, and there was a picture of it during the opening credits of National Lampoon's "Vacation" movie, this is a RS.

Camping

Lake Bemidji SP
7.5 miles north of Bemidji
on a bike path (see directions
in text)

*Oak Haven Resort
14333 Roosevelt Road
Bemidji, MN
218-335-2092

*Becker's Resort
17048 Wild Rice Drive
Bena, MN
800-348-1329

Lodging

*Hampton Inn
1019 Paul Bunyan Dr. S
Bemidji, MN
218-751-3600

Super 8 Motel
1815 Paul Bunyan NW
Bemidji, MN
218-751-8481

*Oak Haven Resort
and *Becker's Resort
Both have cabins. See
Camping for contact info.

Bike Shops

Itasca Sports Rental
15441 Main Park Drive
Itasca State Park, MN
218-266-2150

Home Place Bike & Ski
524 Paul Bunyan Drive SE
Bemidji, MN
218-751-3456

Itasca State Park to Bena (79 miles)

Miles N/S	Directions	Dist	S	T	Services	Miles S/N
0	R onto Park Drive	0.2	0	L		79
0	L onto CR 122 / N Entrance Dr	0.7	0	L		79
1	S onto CR 2 (Cross SH 200)	6.4	3	L		78
	*Cross the MR			L		
7	R onto CR 40/CR 9	7.6	2	L	R	71
	*Cross the MR			L		
15	L onto CR 3	7.1	2	L		64
22	Veer L onto CR 7	6.7	5	M		57
	*Cross MR					
29	R at intersection on CR 7 / 5th St	2.8	5	H	QR	50
	*Bemidji				LQR	
32	R onto Bemidji Ave/Paul Bunyan DR	1.3	0	H		47
33	L onto 1st ST	1.1	8	H		46
34	R onto Lake Ave NE	0.5	0	H		45
34	L onto Roosevelt RD / CR 8	10.4	8	M	CLQ	44
	*Cross MR					
45	L onto CR 33	6	0	L		34
	*Cross MR					
51	R at SS onto CR 12	5.1	2	L	R	28
56	R at SS on CR 39 (*Pennington)	5.7	0		CQ	23
	*Cross MR					
62	L onto CR 91	1.1	4	L		17
63	S on CR 54 (later signed CR 91 again).	11.6	4	L	C	16
74	L at SS on US 2	4.4	8	M	CQ	4
	*Bena				CQ	
79	L onto CR 9					0

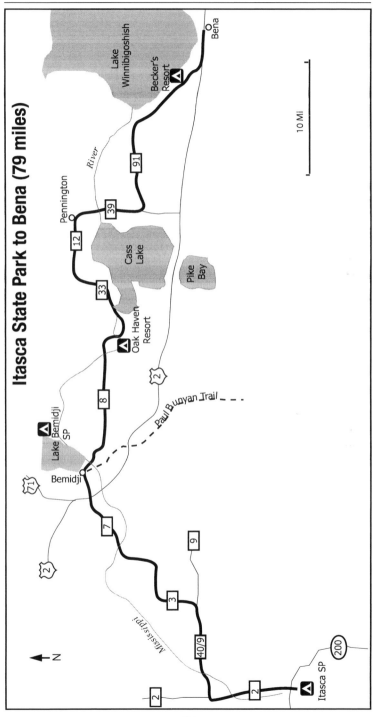

Itasca State Park to Bena (79 miles)

Minnesota: Section 2
Bena to Palisade (99 miles)

After a short ride on US 2, you're back into the forest once again on CR 9. This is another quiet rural road closely bordered on each side by dense trees. The Minnesota DOT has plans to extend the shoulder. Once this has been completed, this will be one sweet ride. The services on this road are located near the end, where you'll find camping, lodging, and a restaurant within the same general area.

CR 39 passes Ball Club Lake, but after that the MRT leads you away from the lake resort region you've been riding through. Other than the area around Grand Rapids, you'll still be riding county roads with little traffic. You won't have your pick of resorts to camp at in this section, but there are still enough options for pitching your tent. Schoolcraft State Park is a good place to camp. The river runs right through the park. If you don't feel comfortable riding the half-mile gravel and dirt road entrance to the park, it isn't so far that you can't walk your bike.

While riding across Minnesota, it is interesting to read the names on the mailboxes. Some of the names you'll see are of Irish, Scandinavian, Swedish, Norwegian, German and other European descent, strong hardworking immigrants who settled here and harvested the state's hardwood forests to supply the wood products needed by a young, fast-growing country.

As you approach Grand Rapids, you ride past the Forest History Center, which will explain more about this. The Center includes an interpretive area with exhibits, films, and displays showing the important role Minnesota played in early America. There is also a "living history" logging camp with interpreters dressed in lumberjack clothing performing tasks of early loggers. The camp includes a camp cook, blacksmith, and wood butcher. Visitors even get a chance to join the crew of "river pigs" (log drivers) as they maneuver logs downriver to the mill. It's a good place to take a break and learn something at the same time.

Grand Rapids offers full services and is a great place to replenish your supplies. Turn right at the intersection of Golf Course Road and Pokegama Avenue and within a half-mile you'll find a laundromat, restaurants, a grocery, and a Wal-Mart®. Continue a half-mile past Wal-Mart® and you'll find the motels I have listed at the end of the section. If you're looking for camping, turn left back at the intersection and follow Pokegama Avenue north for a mile, then turn left on US 2 for about 3 miles to the Pokegama Dam & Rec Area.

About 20 miles after leaving Grand Rapids, at the intersection of CR 10 and SH 200, you'll need to make a decision. Currently there are three different 6-mile stretches of the MRT between SH 200 and Crosby that are gravel. Their locations are described in the Mileage Log. These are hard-packed dirt and gravel roads that I wouldn't recommend for tires smaller than 700/32. If you have the tires for this, I highly recommend taking the MRT route. This is a nice ride. If your bike tires are too small for the gravel section of the MRT, you may want to take the alternate route (described below). Either way, both the MRT and the alternate route pass through Palisade, a small, quaint rural town that is well-equipped for an overnight stay for cyclists.

Before beginning your journey, check the status of the gravel sections of road with the Aitkin County Highway Department (218-927-3741). You will definitely want to follow the MRT once the roads are paved. There is very limited traffic as the route takes you past small farms and woodlands. This is a great opportunity for viewing wildlife. I spotted several deer and turkeys. You get your first sighting of the MR in quite a few miles as the road runs right alongside it. The river has grown a little but is still quite picturesque. As I mentioned before, Palisade has a great setup for cyclists. The Berglund Park campground is right on the MR bank. It has clean showers and restrooms. Downtown is just up the street where you can have a cooked meal and pick up supplies. I rate this a RS. I know it is going to be a favorite stop with cyclists. If only the north section of gravel has been paved at the time of your ride, you could join the alternate route in Palisade, to bypass the remaining gravel segments.

If you choose to bypass this section, your alternate route is to turn left onto SH 200 for about one-and-a-half miles to SH 65. You pass a small rest area with a toilet, and if you need a snack there is a convenience store at the 200/65 intersection. Turn right to follow SH 65 for 21 miles, then right onto SH 232. After 9 miles you will reach Palisade.

Railroad bridge across the Mississippi River next to Berglund Park Campground.

Camping

Tamarat Point CG
3.8 miles off County Road 9
(gravel road)

Pokegama Dam Rec CG
34385 W Hwy 2
Grand Rapids, MN
218-326-6128

*Winnie Dam Rec Area
County Road 9
218-335-8600

Jacobson Campground
1 mile off CR 10
(gravel road)

*Schoolcraft SP
County Road 74
Calumet, MN
218-247-7215

*Berglund Park CG
County Road 10
Palisade, MN

Lodging

*Little Winnie Resort
55671 County Rd 9
Deer River, MN
800-346-8501

Super 8 Motel
1702 S Pokegama Ave
Grand Rapids, MN
218-327-1108

Morning Glory B&B
726 Second Ave
Grand Rapids, MN
218-326-3978

*Gosh Dam Place
38589 Hwy 46
Deer River, MN
218-246-8202

Sawmill Inn
2301 S Pokegama Ave
Grand Rapids, MN
218-326-8501

Alternate Route Lodging
40 Club Inn
950 2nd St NW
Aitkin, MN
218-927-7090

*Ball Club Lake Lodge
34858 County Road 39
Deer River, MN
218-246-8908

AmericInn
1812 S Pokegama Ave
Grand Rapids, MN
800-396-5007

Alternate Route Lodging
Country Inn
115 Front St E
Deerwood, MN
218-534-3101

Bike Shops

Itasca Bike Ski & Fitness
316 NE 4th
Grand Rapids, MN
218-326-1716

Bena to Palisade (99 miles)

Miles N/S	Directions	Dist	S	T	Services	Miles S/N
0	L onto CR 9	11.2	3	M	CL	99
11	R at SS onto SH 46	1.5	4	H	LQR	87
13	R onto CR 39	7.5	3		CL	86
20	L at SS on US 2	1.9	8	M	Q	78
22	R onto CR 18/CR 3 (veers L)	9	2	L		77
31	R onto CR 74	3.2	2		C	68
	*Schoolcraft SP(1/2 mile on dirt road)				C	
34	L at SS onto CR 65	2.7	2	M		64
37	L onto SH 6	1.7	1	M		62
39	R onto CR 64/CR 63	7.3	3	M		60
46	Bike path along CR 63	1.5	P			
48	R at SS onto CR 76	1.9	8	M		51
49	L at SS onto CR 23/Golf Course Rd/10th St SE (*Grand Rapids)	2.3	8	H	CGQR	49
52	L at roundabout onto 7th AVE	0.4	3	H	Q	47
52	R onto River Road/CR 3	18.3	8	M	Q	47
70	S as CR 3 becomes CR 10	2.3	8	M		28
73	S at SS CR 10 (*See text for alternate route SH 200/ SH 65)	8.2	0			26
81	CR 10 becomes gravel	6.7	0			18
88	CR 10 is paved once again.	11	3			11
99	S at SS on CR 10 (*Palisade)		0	L	CQR	0

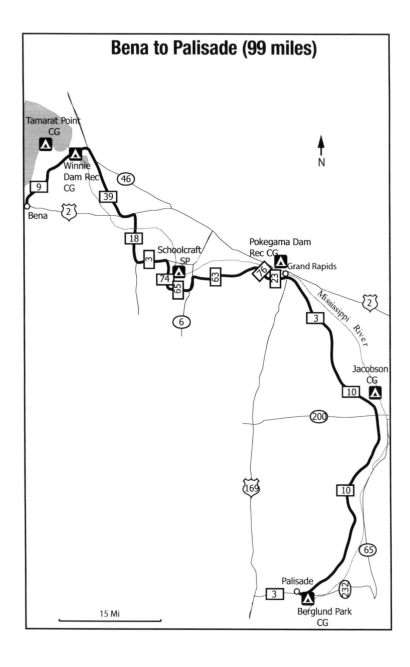

Bena to Palisade (99 miles)

Tamarat Point CG

Winnie Dam Rec CG

46

39

9

2 Bena

18

3

Schoolcraft SP

74

65

63

6

Pokegama Dam Rec CG

76

23

Grand Rapids

Mississippi River

2

3

N

Jacobson CG

10

200

169

10

65

Palisade

3

232

Berglund Park CG

15 Mi

Minnesota: Section 3
Palisade to Charles Lindbergh State Park (88 miles)

The MRT leaves Palisade on CR 10. At the time of this writing, there is another 6-mile section of gravel on this next stretch. You won't have to ride far to check the status of the road, because it begins just outside of town. If the road is still gravel, and you prefer not to ride on it, the alternate route is to follow CR 3 west out of Palisade for about 5 miles, then turn left onto US 169. After about 2 miles on US 169, you'll rejoin the MRT where CR 10 emerges.

For those who continue out of Palisade on CR 10, which is also the Great River Road, you're in for more of the same scenery you saw on CR 10 north of Palisade. The route meanders through the Minnesota countryside, with quaint farms, patches of dense forests, glimpses of the MR, and plenty of wildlife viewing opportunities.

The MRT only stays on US 169 for just over a mile before turning right onto CR 21. The first part of this road is the final stretch of gravel. The Minnesota DOT has plans for paving all three sections, so this may not be an issue on your ride. But if it is still gravel, and you prefer not to ride on gravel, the alternate route is to continue south on US 169 for another 12 miles to Atkins (lodging is available at the 40 Club Inn Motel, 218-927-7090), then continue another 14 miles on SH 210 to Crosby. At this point you will rejoin the MRT with all the gravel sections behind you. For those continuing to follow the MRT route on CR 21, bid a hearty farewell to the heavy traffic on US 169 and enjoy a peaceful ride in this rural setting.

Crosby refers to itself as the "Antique Capital of the Lakes Area" and has several specialty stores to back it up. There are also several places to eat in town, as well as a city campground. If you are not camping, and you're ready to stop for the day, your lodging choices are limited to one. But even if there were a dozen places to stay, the Nordic Inn Medieval Brew and Bed would be at the top of the list. The converted old Methodist Church serves as an interactive theater and bed & breakfast, with your host, "The Crazy Viking." As you can imagine, there is an interesting story behind the origin of the Inn. I'll allow the host to share it with you.

As you enter Brainerd, the MRT turns off the main highway and weaves through neighborhoods, bypassing the heavy traffic. This initial turn is easy to miss. Watch for the turn onto 13th Avenue just after SH 210 loses the shoulder and gains a median.

Follow the Mileage Log closely through Brainerd. There are a lot of turns. On 1st Street, there are train tracks running right down the middle of the street. It would be interesting to witness the effect a train running down the middle of the road would have on vehicles using the road.

The MRT routes you through downtown Brainerd. On Laurel Street quaint bars and restaurants provide a welcome break. There is a pedestrian walkway on College Drive you can use to cross the MR. At the stop light, after crossing the river, College Drive becomes College Road. On the left side of the road is another pedestrian walk. You can use this walkway to avoid the heavy traffic. After about a mile on College Road, you'll come to a stop light for SH 371. If you are planning to ride the Paul Bunyan Trail loop back to Bemidji, turn right on SH 371, ride about $1^1/_2$ miles, then turn right on Excelsior Road to the PBT trailhead. Refer to the alternate route section, at the end of the chapter, for a description of this route.

To continue on the MRT, cross the pedestrian walkway at the intersection, and follow the paved bike path paralleling SH 371. The path winds around through a residential neighborhood, providing a pleasant break from the traffic you've been riding in. If you don't mind heavy traffic, you have the option of turning left at the stop light onto SH 371, because the bike path rejoins the highway another 3 miles south. There is a Wal-Mart® at the start of the bike path and also nearby eating places.

When the bike path returns to SH 371, you pass through a gate. Follow the paved path under the highway, curve up the other side to cross a bridge, and then curve under the highway again to come out on the southbound side of the highway. There are plans to extend the bike path to Crow Wing State Park, but for now the paved path ends here. You will need to push your bike up the bank of the highway, then continue south on SH 371. This is a busy four-lane highway but you have an 8-foot shoulder.

The turn for Crow Wing State Park is about 5 miles after you rejoin SH 371. The park is bordered by the MR and wooded forest, providing an ideal wildlife habitat. I was fortunate enough to see a flock of about 60 turkeys when I camped there. There are also interpretative exhibits explaining the area's history, including a boardwalk through the former town site of the Old Crow Wing Village. Like most Minnesota state parks, the campground includes showers.

Across from the entrance to Crow Wing State Park is a rest

area that has a computer with free Internet access. This is a good opportunity for you to catch up on your e-mail.

When reaching Little Falls, you can turn left on Broadway and cross the MR for a larger selection of services. As you continue on CR 52, the Charles Lindbergh State Park is just outside of Little Falls. This is another convenient camping site right on the MRT. Be sure to take advantage of this because it's the last non-commercial camping for quite a while.

The park includes tours of the boyhood home of the world-renowned pilot, plus the Lindbergh Visitor Center, which covers the lives of three generations of Lindberghs in Minnesota. Next to the park is the Charles A. Weyerhaeuser Museum. The free museum covers the history of the area from the time Indians resided there through the early settler period. Knowing the history of an area makes the ride more interesting. As I'm riding across a state, I like to reflect on an area's history and try to imagine what it was like back then. On some of the more remote county roads, it's not that difficult to visualize.

Camping

Crosby Memorial Park	Crow Wing SP	Charles Lindbergh SP
2nd St SW	5 miles south of Brainerd	1615 Lindbergh Dr S
Crosby, MN	on SH 371	Little Falls, MN
218-546-5021	218-825-3075	320-616-2525

Lodging

Nordic Inn	Downtown Motel	Red Roof Inn
210 First Ave NW	507 S 6th St	2115 S 6th
Crosby, MN	Brainerd, MN	Brainerd, MN
218-546-8299	218-829-4789	888-562-2944
Whiteley Creek B&B	Waller House B&B	Super 8 Motel
12349 Whiteley Cr Trail	301 Third Street SE	300 12th St NE
Brainerd, MN	Little Falls, MN	Little Falls, MN
218-829-0654	320-632-2836	320-632-2351

Bike Shops

Easy Rider Bike Shop	Trailblazer Bikes	Fast Bikes
415 Washington St	24 Washington St	1419 Rosewood St
Brainerd, MN	Brainerd, MN	Brainerd, MN
218-829-5516	218-829-8542	218-829-0115
	(one block from PBT)	

Palisade to Charles Lindbergh State Park (88 miles)

Miles N/S	Directions	Dist	S	T	Services	Miles S/N
0	S at SS on CR 10 (*Palisade)	0.3	0	L	CQR	88
0	CR 10 becomes gravel	6.7	0	L		88
7	L onto US 169 (gravel ends at 169)	1.3	2	H		81
8	R onto CR 21 (gravel)	6.5	0	L		80
15	L at SS onto CR 1/Osprey Ave	2	2	M		74
17	R onto CR 22	3.8	2	M		72
21	CR 22 turns L then becomes CR 11 after 6 tenths of a mile.	11.1	0	M		68
32	L at SS onto SH 6	4.8	4	H	R	57
37	S at SS onto SH 210	13.8	8	H		52
	*Crosby				CGLQR	
50	R onto 13th Ave NE	0	0	L	Q	38
	*Brainerd				GLQR	
50	L onto H St.	0.9	0	L		38
51	L onto 1st Ave NE	0.1	0	L		37
51	R onto Evergreen Ave/Fir St	0.3	0	L		37
52	L onto N 8th St	0.6	0	M	QR	37
52	R onto Laurel St	0.5	0	M	R	36
53	L onto East River Rd (bike path)	0.7	P	L		36
53	R at SS onto College Dr (Crosses MR)	0.8	3	H		35
54	S at SL onto College Rd (bike path)	1.1	P	H	Q	34
55	L onto bike path (across SH 371)	2.3	P	L	GR	33
58	L at SS on the bike path (parallel Jasperwood Dr)	0.9	P	L		31
59	Pass thru the gate bordering SH 371	0	P	L		30
59	Follow the path under the bridge to circle around to cross the MR.	0.1	P	L		30
59	After circling back under the bridge, now on the west side, walk your bike up to join SH 371 south.	18.6	8	H	CR	30
	*R to Crow Wing SP(1 mile paved).				C	
77	R onto SH 115.	1.6	3	M		11
79	L onto CR 213	5.7	2	M	Q	10
85	L at SS continuing on CR 213	0.3	0	M		4
85	R onto CR 13	0.1	2	M		4
85	L at SS onto CR 52	1.7	8	M		4
87	S at SL on CR 52	1.8	0	M		2
	*Little Falls				GLQR	
88	*Charles Lindbergh SP				C	0

Palisade to Charles Lindbergh SP (88 miles)

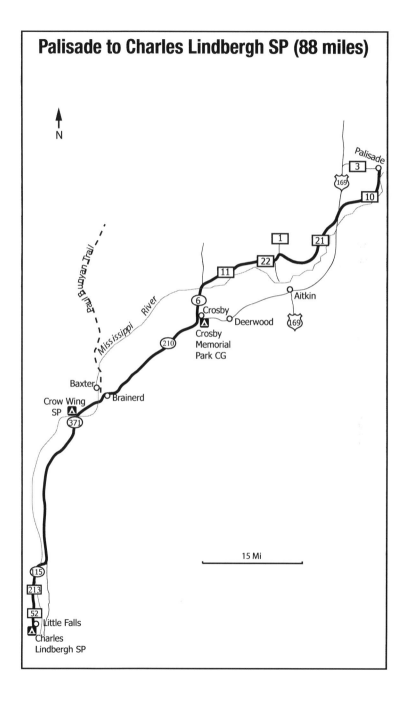

N

Palisade
3
169
10
1
21
22
11
6
Aitkin
Crosby
Deerwood
169
Crosby
Memorial
Park CG
210
Mississippi River
Paul Bunyan Trail
Baxter
Crow Wing
SP
Brainerd
371
15 Mi
115
213
52
Little Falls
Charles
Lindbergh SP

Minnesota: Section 4
Charles Lindbergh SP to Coon Rapids Dam (91 miles)

After Charles Lindbergh State Park, the next major highlight on the MRT is St. Cloud. The highway approaching the city runs alongside the MR with a painted bike lane. It is easy to miss the turn onto the CR 29 bridge because there are no signs on Riverside Avenue for the bridge. If you follow the distance on the Mileage Log, you'll know when to look for the bridge and should have no problem identifying it. Once you have crossed the MR and are on Benton Drive, you'll need to use the Mileage Log distance once again to identify the turn to the beginning of Island View Park Trail. There is no street sign for this turn either. The road off of Benton Drive crosses a railroad track to a mobile home park. As soon as you cross the tracks, turn left. At the end of this road, as it curves right, the paved bike trail continues straight.

The MRT does an excellent job of routing you through St. Cloud. Overall, it avoids heavy traffic and provides a scenic ride with a view of the river. The route doesn't take you past a variety of eating places, so you will need to check out side streets to find what you want. The adjoining Munsinger and Clemens Gardens on Killian Boulevard is a definite RS. If possible, plan your lunch stop here. This is a very relaxing setting.

After passing the St. Cloud University campus, the city gives you a nice send-off on the Beaver Island Trail. This is a pleasant 2-mile paved bike path through dense woods. After leaving the trail the route isn't so pleasant. CR 75 has heavy traffic and not much of a shoulder. But help is on the way. The Minnesota DOT has plans to extend this shoulder. As a matter of fact, the DOT has a very aggressive agenda for improving the entire MRT in the state of Minnesota.

I also want to add, that to reach the Holiday Inn I have listed, follow CR 75 about a mile before turning left onto 43rd Street S, then right for a block on Clearwater Road.

The next services on the MRT are in Monticello. This is also where the route leaves CR 75, turning onto CR 39. Minnesota is pretty good about signing their county roads, so you can generally maneuver through the state using county road names. However, CR 42 and CR 12 are also called Dayton River Road and River Road in the Otsego and Dayton areas. I did not list lodging for this area because they are several miles off the MRT.

The MRT skirts the city of Champlin, but the traffic is still pretty heavy. It helps to use the short bike path on the right side of the road. The ride is also pretty confusing in this busy area when CR12 overlaps US 169 for a short stretch. At the stop light for US 169, veer right for half a mile, then follow CR 12 off to the left to the Coon Rapids Regional Dam.

There are visitor centers and parks on each side of the Coon Rapids dam. Both centers have interpretive displays, restrooms, and picnic areas, providing a pleasant atmosphere to learn more about the history of the area. The MRT crosses over the dam on a pedestrian/bike path.

Camping

St Cloud Campground RV
 2491 2nd St SE
St. Cloud, MN
320-251-4463

Lodging

Gateway Motel
310 Lincoln Ave SE
St. Cloud, MN
320-252-4050

*Riverside Guest Haus B&B
912 Riverside Dr SE
St. Cloud, MN
888-252-2134

Holiday Inn Express
4322 Clearwater Rd
St. Cloud, MN
320-240-8000
(1 mile south on hwy 75)

Heritage House B&B
402 6th Ave S
St. Cloud, MN
888-547-4422

Victorian Oaks B&B
404 9th Ave S
St. Cloud, MN
320-202-1404

*AmericInn Motel
118 E 7th St
Monticello, MN
763-295-4700

Bike Shops

Joe's Bike Shop
225 9th Ave S
Sauk Rapids, MN
320-255-0170

Revolution Cycle & Ski
160 29th Ave
St. Cloud, MN
320-251-2453

Rod's Bike Shop
28 Lincoln Ave
St. Cloud, MN
320-259-1964

Fitzharris Bike & Sport
105 7th Ave
St. Cloud, MN
320-251-2844

Erike's Bike Shop
2115 W Division St
St. Cloud, MN
320-257-0111

Charles Lindbergh SP to Coon Rapids Dam (91 miles)

Miles N/S	Directions	Dist	S	T	Services	Miles S/N
	*Charles Lindbergh SP				C	
0	S onto CR 52	9.8	0	M		91
10	S at SS onto CR 25	1.7	0	M		82
12	L onto CR 21/CR 1	6.5	0	M		80
18	R at SS continue on CR 1/Riverside Ave	10.4	5	M		73
28	R on bike path after riding under CR 29 bridge	0.1	P	L		63
29	R at YS onto CR 29 bridge (cross MR)	0.2	8	M		63
29	R on Benton DR	0.9	8	M	R	63
	*Sauk Rapids				GQR	
30	R on Island View Park Trail (See text)	0.3	P	L		62
30	Turn right on River Ave S	2.1	0	M	R	62
32	River Ave curves left to become 12th St	0.1	0	H		59
32	R at SS on Broadway Ave/Riverside DR	0.9	0	H		59
	*St. Cloud				CGLQR	
33	L onto 1st St	0	0	M		58
33	R onto 2nd Ave	0.2	0	M		58
33	S at SL on Riverside Dr	1.1	0	M		58
34	L onto 13th St	0	0	M		57
34	R at SS onto Killian Blvd	0.3	0	H		57
35	R at SL onto University Blvd/Michigan Ave (cross MR)	0.7	P	H		57
35	L at SL onto 5th Ave	0.4	0	H		56
36	L onto 15th St	0	0	M		56
36	R onto 3rd Ave	0.1	0	M		56
36	S onto Beaver Island Trail	2.3	P	L		56
38	L at SL onto CR 75/Roosevelt Rd	2.2	3	H		53
40	L onto CR 75	1.8	3	H		51
42	L at SL on CR 75	19.1	0	M		49
	*Monticello				GLQR	
61	R on bike path	1.8	P	L		30
63	Bike lane ends continue on CR 75	1.4	2	M		28
64	L at SL onto CR 39/95th St/ 90th St	14.4	8	H		27
79	R onto CR 42/CR 12	5.9	1	M	QR	13
	(*Dayton)				QR	
	(*Champlin)				QR	
85	R on bike path	1.7	P	H		7
86	R at SL onto CR 12/US 169	0.4	0	H		5
87	L at SL onto CR 12	3.6	0	H		5
90	L onto W River Rd	1	4	H		1
91	Coon Rapids Dam Regional Park					0

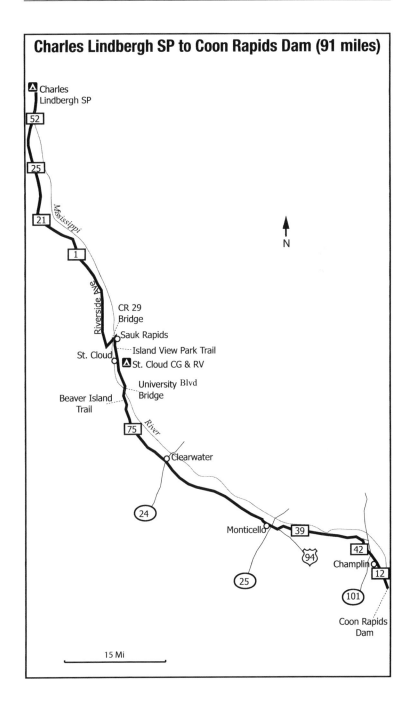

Charles Lindbergh SP to Coon Rapids Dam (91 miles)

- Charles Lindbergh SP
- 52
- 25
- Mississippi
- 21
- 1
- Riverside Ave
- N
- CR 29 Bridge
- Sauk Rapids
- Island View Park Trail
- St. Cloud
- St. Cloud CG & RV
- University Blvd Bridge
- Beaver Island Trail
- 75
- River
- Clearwater
- 24
- Monticello
- 39
- 94
- 42
- Champlin
- 12
- 25
- 101
- Coon Rapids Dam
- 15 Mi

Minnesota: Section 5
Coon Rapids Dam to Inver Grove Heights (39 miles)

On the east side of the river, at Coon Rapids Regional Dam, the MRT follows the Mississippi Regional Trail Corridor (MRTC). This signed bike trail utilizes bike paths and roads to weave through neighborhoods and alongside parks on the east side of the MR. At the time I last rode the MRTC, most of the turns were marked with either MRTC or MRT signs. But signs have a way of disappearing, so keep the Mileage Log close at hand to avoid unintended side trips. You get your first view of the Minneapolis skyline while riding NE Marshall Street.

As I was planning my ride through the Minneapolis and St. Paul area, I was concerned about the traffic and complex series of directions generally associated with cycling through most major cities. However, for these beautiful cities my concerns were unwarranted. With the MRT utilizing the bike trails on both the east and west banks of the river, this is a really enjoyable bike ride.

After crossing the Plymouth Bridge, you have the pleasure of riding one of the true jewels of the MRT, the Grand Rounds Scenic Byway (GRSB). This is a fantastic pedestrian/bike path running along the west bank of the MR. You ride past St. Anthony Falls, Stone Bridge, a memorial commemorating the location of the first bridge across the MR, the famous Grain Belt beer sign, historic markers, interpretive displays and parks, just to mention a few of the attractions. Take your time riding this stretch. Read about the history of the river in the area. It is interesting to discover the threat St. Anthony Falls had once been to navigation on the river, and how erosion by the river's swift currents and the increased logging of the numerous mills has moved the falls a mile farther downriver from where it was when Father Hennepin first saw it in 1680. This section is truly a RS. If you want to tour the area properly, I suggest a stop at the visitor center to plan your activities. The center is located in the Convention & Group Tourism office at 250 Marquette Avenue, Suite 1300, 800-445-7412. To get to their office, after about a mile on the GRSB turn right on Hennepin Avenue, then left on 1st Street for about a block, then right on Marquette Avenue. The area around the visitor center also offers a good choice of eating places. This will also put you only a couple of blocks away from The Residence Inn and Courtyard by Marriott, which I listed as lodging for Minneapolis. The One on One Bicycle Studio is also nearby if you need repairs or parts. This neighborhood has all of the ingredients to make this a choice area to spend some time.

Minneapolis and St. Paul have numerous bike trails. These trails offer a variety of options for you to plan alternate side trips in the area, or to even plan your own route through the cities. The MRT has plans to mark these routes on both sides of the river. Even though I expanded the scale of the map for this section to provide greater detail, I still did not have room to include all of the area trails. However, I believe the MRT route printed in the section map and outlined in the Mileage Log does provides cyclists a route that includes the best trails for both sides of the river, while providing an easy-to-follow route through the Twin Cities.

After crossing the Ford Bridge to the east side of the MR, the MRT takes you through what was originally the 160-acre farm of English immigrant Thomas Crosby. It is a nature park now. The paved bike path meanders through the dense woodlands of the park and along the banks of the river. A few miles after exiting the nature park, you will climb a small hill to downtown St. Paul. The MRT takes you right past the St. Paul Convention & Visitors Authority at 175 West Kellogg Boulevard, Suite 502, 651-265-4900. Be sure to stop and let the experts help you plan your visit. The small park located on the east side of the Wabasha Bridge is a good place to pause for a break to enjoy a great view of the MR with Minneapolis in the distance.

With its large ethnically diverse population and cultural heritage, St. Paul offers some unique attractions for visitors. You'll experience some of this diverse heritage, once again back on the west bank of the MR, as you ride through a neighborhood of brightly painted restaurants offering authentic Mexican food. I recommend timing your eating schedule accordingly to take advantage of this dining opportunity.

After leaving St. Paul, watch for the Simon Ravine Trailhead parking lot on the west side of Concord Street. This is the northern end of the South St. Paul Regional Trail. This is a paved bike/ pedestrian trail that offers cyclists a break from the traffic, as it takes you on top of the levee for an unobstructed view of the MR.

Camping
N/A

Lodging

Residence Inn
425 S. 2nd St
Minneapolis, MN
612-340-1300

Courtyard by Marriott
225 South 3rd Ave
Minneapolis, MN
612-375-1700

Best Western Downtown
405 South 8th St
Minneapolis, MN
800-373-3131

Coe Carriage House B&B
1700 Third Ave South
Minneapolis, MN
612-871-4249

Minneapolis Grand Hotel
615 2nd Ave South
Minneapolis, MN
612-339-3655

Radisson Riverfront
11 East Kellogg Blvd
St. Paul, MN
651-292-1900

Bike Shops

One on One Bike Studio
117 Washington Ave N.
Minneapolis, MN
612-371-9565
(close to MRT)

Freewheel Bike
1812 South 6Th St
Minneapolis, MN
612-339-2235
(close to MRT)

Erik's Bike & Boards
1312 4th St SE
Minneapolis, MN
612-617-8002

Alternative Bike Shop
3013 Lyndale Ave S
Minneapolis, MN
612-374-3635

Grand Performance
1938 Grand Ave
St. Paul, MN
651-699-2640

Now Bike & Fitness
75 Snelling Ave N
St. Paul, MN
651-644-2354

Coon Rapids Dam to Inver Grove Heights (39 miles)

Miles N/S	Directions	Dist	S	T	Services	Miles S/N
0	R onto (MRTC) after crossing the dam.	1.8	P	L		39
2	R onto Mississippi Blvd	0.6	0	L		37
2	R at the trail crossing sign onto MRTC.	0	0	L		36
2	S 1 block later onto Broad Ave	0.1	0	L		36
3	R onto Kimbal St	0	0	L		36
3	L onto Riverview Terrace	0.7	0	L		36
3	Follow sign to return to MRTC trail.	0.2	P	L		35
3	R onto Alden Way after a small hill	0.6	0	L		35
4	Curve L onto 75th Way	0.2	0	L		35
4	R onto bike path after crossing East River Rd	1.1	P	L		34
5	L onto Rice Creek Way	0.3	0	L		33
6	L onto MRTC at the intersection of Rice Creek and Ashton Ave (then immediate R turn because L is the Rice Cr Trail)	1	P	L		33
7	S at SL to cross East River Rd	0.2	P	L		32
7	Cross Anna Ave to follow MRTC trail past Island of Peace County Park	0.4	P	L		32
7	S at SL	0.3	P	L		31
8	Veer R at fork in bike path to ride under the bridge.	2.7	P	L		31
10	Curve R at SL for NE 37 Ave	0.4	P	L		28

11	S on bike path across St Anthony Pkwy	0.5	P	L		28
11	R at SL onto NE Marshall St	2.3	0	L		27
13	R on NE 8th Ave, to cross the MR on Plymouth Bridge.	0.1	P	H		25
	*Minneapolis				GLQR	
14	Curve R to ride under bridge to the Grand Round Scenic Byway	7.7	P	L		25
21	L at sign for Lock and Dam # 1 then climb a small hill to Ford bridge.	0.2	P	L		17
21	L onto Ford Bridge (cross MR)	0.1	P	H		17
22	Curve L immediately after crossing the MR to ride under the bridge along the Mississippi River Blvd	2.4	P	H		17
24	At the fork in the bike path veer L to take the bridge over the highway	0.1	P	H		15
24	Just after passing through a SL turn R onto the bike path bordering Crosby Farm Road	0.3	P	L		15
24	Veer R onto bike path into the woods.	2.1	P	L		14
26	R at SL onto Sheppard Rd	0.1	P	H		12
27	Veer L as the bike trail forks, crossing the highway ramp to ride under the overpass.	3.9	P	H		12
30	L at SL onto Eagle Parkway and Old Chestnut St.	0.4	P	M		8
31	R at the top of hill onto Kellogg Blvd	0.3	P	H		8
31	S at SL across Market St	0.2	P	H	R	7
	*St. Paul				GLQR	
31	R onto Wabasha St bridge (cross MR)	0.8	P	H		7
32	Wabasha St curves L to become Cesar Chevez	1.1	4	H		6
33	Cesar Chevez becomes Concord St.	1.2	6	H	R	5
34	R at the Simon Ravine Trailhead parking lot to take the bike overpass to begin the South St Paul Regional Trail	4.1	P	L		4
39	L onto Richmond Ave (end of bike path).					0

Native American sculpture at the trailhead for South St. Paul Regional Trail.

33

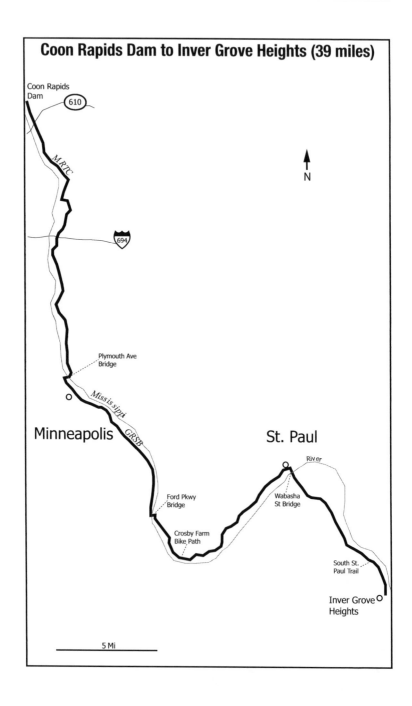

Coon Rapids Dam to Inver Grove Heights (39 miles)

Coon Rapids
Dam

610

MRTC

N

694

Plymouth Ave
Bridge

Mississippi

Minneapolis

GRSB

St. Paul

River

Ford Pkwy
Bridge

Wabasha
St Bridge

Crosby Farm
Bike Path

South St.
Paul Trail

Inver Grove
Heights

5 Mi

Minnesota: Section 6
Inver Grove Heights to Kellogg (90 miles)

For those cyclists interested in a 200-mile-plus loop tour on the MRT, I highly recommend crossing the MR from Hastings to Prescott, then following the Wisconsin MRT south to La Crosse. At that point, you can cross back to the west side of the river to La Crescent, then return on the MRT to Hastings. Both river crossings are biker-friendly. By riding in a clockwise direction, you will be on the river side of the route, with the best views. Whether you prefer campgrounds, motels, or bed-and-breakfasts you shouldn't have a problem locating accommodations. There are also plenty of eating establishments on the route. I'm sure it will be a memorable ride for you.

If you are not taking the suggested loop, continue instead on Section 6. This stretch of the MRT takes you on some busy roads in the beginning. I recently learned from the DOT of plans for a bike path that will bypass this section. The trail is still in the planning stages, but when finished, it will provide an almost continuous bike path from the South St. Paul Regional Trail all the way to Hastings. In the interim, follow the directions in the Mileage Log, adjust your mirror, keep an eye on the traffic, and stay safe.

On the outskirts of Hastings, the MRT follows the Hastings Trail System. This is almost a 3-mile paved trail that takes you along a wetland area, offering great waterfowl viewing opportunities. You will also pass an interesting historical marker. It explains how the downtown business owners in Hastings were concerned that a new bridge across the MR would elevate the approaching highway above the downtown district. They feared this would cut their businesses off from the normal traffic flow. To avoid this, the design of the bridge was changed to include a spiral ramp, which would continue routing traffic through the downtown area. I think that would have been something to see. However, the spiral ramp was replaced when the current bridge was constructed.

In Hastings, if you are in need of services, the best selection of restaurants and grocery stores is on south SH 61. The motel I have listed is also on this road. If you take this detour, to resume the ride, turn east on 10th Street and it will take you back onto the MRT.

As you approach SH 61 on CR18, brace yourself for the only climb on the MRT in Minnesota. Originally there was a second, much longer climb, when the MRT routed you by the Great River Bluffs State Park. The route has recently been revised, eliminating this second climb. The Great River Bluffs State Park is now on an MRT alternate route. The entrance to the park includes a 2-mile gravel road. I rode the original route on my first ride through here. It is a beautiful ride that follows the Apple Blossom Scenic Drive. There are beautiful mountain top views of the MR, and the descent into La Crescent is a blast.

Traffic is very heavy on SH 61, but there is a good shoulder. Be sure to watch for the turn for the Cannon Valley Trail. There are two opportunities to join the bike trail. The first is also a turn for the A.P. Anderson Park ball fields. Follow the signs through the park and veer left at any intersection. The second entrance to the trail is at Lower A.P. Anderson Park. Once you're on the bike path, it will take you all the way into Red Wing.

When you reach the end of the bike trail, if you are in need of services, turn right. This will take you to the newer section of Red Wing, with grocery stores, fast food restaurants, lodging, etc. If you are in need of a bike shop, when you reach the intersection of Old West Main Street and Withers Harbor Drive, continue straight on Old West Main Street another mile, to The Route bike shop. If you do stop at the bike shop, be sure to let them know you are riding the MRT. For that matter, every place you spend money, let them know you are riding the MRT. Promote the trail and cycling, whenever possible.

Red Wing has a thriving downtown area with shops, restaurants, coffee shops, and galleries. I really enjoy peddling around these well-preserved downtown historic districts. If you are spending the night, you might want to stay at the historic St. James Hotel on Main Street. This elegant hotel was built in 1875. All of its rooms are named after riverboats that once were piloted on the MR.

When you reach Lake City, the MRT routes you along the shores of Lake Pepin. My first thought was that the huge lake was formed by a man-made dam. However, there is a historical marker along the route that explains how the lake was naturally formed, and how it was an important route used by Native Americans.

In the summer of 1922, 18-year-old Ralph Samuelson came to Lake Pepin to work on his idea of creating a way to ski on water the way you can ski on snow. He tried using wooden barrel slats and snow skis, before successfully fashioning pine boards with upturned ends. Samuelson is officially recognized as the inventor of water skis, but he failed to patent his invention. Three years later, Fred Waller patented the Dolphin Akwa-Skees.

Camping

Greenwood Campground
13797 190th St E
Hastings, MN
651-437-5269

*Lake Pepin CG
1818 High St. N
Lake City, MN
651-345-2909

*Frontenac SP
29223 County 28 Blvd
Frontenac, MN
651-345-3401

City of Wabasha Rec
900 Hiawatha Dr
Wabasha, MN
651-565-4568

*Hok-Si-La CG
2500 N Hwy 61
Lake City, MN
651-345-3855

Lodging

Hastings Inn
1520 Vermillion St
Hastings, MN
651-437-3155

*Round Barn Farm B&B
28650 Wildwood Lane
Red Wing, MN
651-385-9250

*Super 8 Motel
232 Wither Harbor Dr.
Red Wing, MN
651-388-0491

*Sunset Motel
1515 N Lakeshore Dr
Lake City, MN
651-345-5331

*St. James Hotel
406 Main Street
Red Wing, MN
800-252-1875

*Bridgewaters B&B
136 Bridge Avenue
Wabasha, MN
651-565-4208

Bike Shops

The Route
200 Second St East
Hastings, MN
651-437-4010

The Route
1932 Old West Main St
Red Wing, MN
651-388-1082

River Rider Cycle
257 Main St West
Wabasha, MN
651-565-4834

Inver Grove Heights to Kellogg (90 miles)

Miles N/S	Directions	Dist	S	T	Services	Miles S/N
0	L onto Richmond Ave (end of bike path).	0.2	0	L		90
0	L at SL onto Concord St.	1.5	4	H	QR	90
2	L onto 66th St (1 block)	0	0	M	R	88
2	R onto River Rd	1.2	0	H		88
3	R onto 77th St.	0.2	0	H		87
3	L onto Dickman Trail (not a bike trail)	0.2	0	H		87
3	L onto Concord Blvd	2.2	0	H		87
5	R onto Courthouse Blvd Ct	0.9	6	H		84
6	L onto Barnes Ave	2.2	0	M		83
9	Veer R onto 105th St	0.3	0	M		81
9	L at SS onto Rich Valley Blvd/Blaine Ave	4.1	1	M		81
13	L at SS onto 145th St/CR 42	3.4	6	H		77
16	R at SS onto Courthouse Blvd/SH 55	1.9	0	H		73
18	L on CR 42/Mississippi Tr/Ninniger Rd	4.2	4	M		72
23	L to begin Hastings Trail System bike path (across from Madison St sign)	0.4	P	L		67

23	L at SS then R at the SS at the bottom.	2.1	P	L		67
25	R onto Tyler St	0.2	0	M		65
	*Hastings				GLQR	
25	L onto 3rd St (1 block)	0	0	M		65
25	R onto Bailly St	0.4	0	M		65
26	L onto Veteran Bikeway (bike path)	0.6	P	L		64
26	L at SS onto E 10th St/CR54/Ravenna Tr	7.8	0	M		64
34	L onto CR68/CR18	8.2	4	M		56
42	L at SS onto US 61	1.9	8	H		48
44	R at Cannondale Rd to begin Cannon Valley Tr bike path (use fee)	4.7	P	L		46
49	L onto Old West Main St(bike path ends)	0.2	0	M	QR	41
	*Red Wing				GLQR	
49	L onto Withers Harbor Dr	0.2	0	M	LR	41
49	S onto Levee Rd	1.2	0	M		41
50	R onto Broad St 1 block/L onto Levee St 1 block/S onto Bush St)	0.2	0	M		39
51	L at SL onto West Main St/US 61	10.6	8	H	LR	39
61	L onto CR2	3.4	0	L	C	29
	*Frontenac SP				C	
65	L at SS onto US 61	4.6	8	H		25
	*Lake City				CGLQR	
69	L onto N Park St	0.1	0	L		21
69	R onto N Franklin St/E Marion St	0.6	0	L		21
70	L onto US 61	11.8	8	H		20
82	L onto 5th Grant Blvd West	1.5	0	L		8
83	L onto Bridge Ave	0.1	0	L	L	7
83	R onto 2nd St West	0.6	0	L		7
	*Wabasha				CGLQR	
84	Curve R onto Pierce Ave	0.1	0	L		6
84	L at SS onto Hiawatha Dr E/CR30	0.6	0	M		6
85	Bike path on the left side of the road.	1.3	P	L		5
86	L onto CR30 (bike path ends)	2.4	0	M		4
88	Curve R then turn L at SS onto US 61	1.1	8	H		2
89	L onto CR18	0.4	0	M		0
90	*Kellogg					0

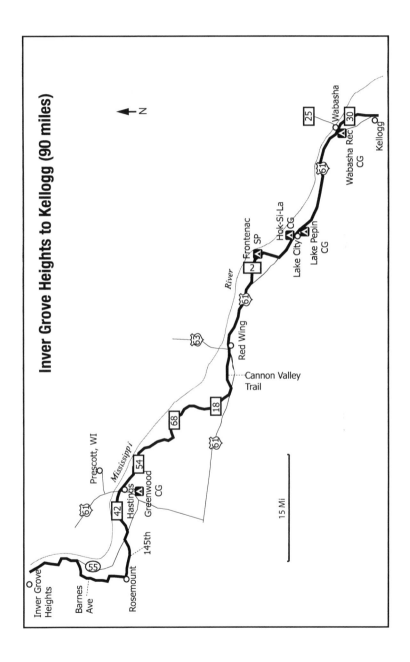

Inver Grove Heights to Kellogg (90 miles)

Minnesota: Section 7
Kellogg to Iowa State Line (82 miles)

Minnesota's scenic bluff region begins in Hastings and extends along the MR to the state's southeastern section. The bluffs are composed of erosion-resistant dolomite formations. Section 7 of the MRT takes you through some of the region's more dramatic formations. At times the bluffs tower over your right shoulder by as much as 500 feet, with the Mississippi River on your left. Together this makes a very scenic ride for the conclusion of your Minnesota MRT tour.

As you leave Minnesota City, the route is slightly confusing. Harbor Drive winds around a short descent, then curves right onto Prairie Island Road, which has no street sign on the northern end. You'll know you're on Prairie Island Road when you see the sign for the Minnesota City Boat Club.

Prairie Island Road has light traffic and runs alongside MR wetlands. I spotted a variety of water fowl feeding in the river's water inlets, and viewed hawks perched in trees in fields on the opposite side of the road. If you would like to spend more time in the area, the Prairie Island Campground is right alongside the road.

As I mentioned earlier, logging was a big business in Minnesota in its early years. After the treaties with Native Americans were signed in the 1830s, investors for the large lumber companies eagerly bought up huge tracts of the thick tall pines that blanketed the state. Large numbers of immigrants from Northern Europe were hired to work in the lumber camps. It took only 40 years to clear out the forests that had taken centuries to grow. With the depletion of the area's primary resource, you would think this would have devastated the state. The results were just the opposite. Once the trees were cleared, it opened the land for settlers to move in. For the cost of just $1.25 an acre, and the promise that they would build dwellings and work the land, pioneers were drawn to the Territory of Minnesota. This surge in the population contributed to the territory's becoming the 32nd state admitted to the Union. This is just a piece of interesting history about the area, to give you something to talk about with your riding partner.

Winona is another picturesque and historic Minnesota town that the MRT routes you through. The course weaves through the downtown district and some of its quaint neighborhoods. As you ride along Fifth Street, watch for the St. Stanislaus Catholic

Church, located on Fourth Street. It would be difficult to miss this enormous structure, with its statues of horn-blowing angels, and other figures perched high on the towers of its roof.

If you are tired of a diet of camp food, and have been waiting to reward yourself with some real food, Winona is a great place to do it. Whether it's pizza, Oriental food, steaks, seafood, or any other style of food you crave, you're sure to find it here. There is also a variety of choices for lodging.

Once again back on US 61, you'll pass the turn to Great River Bluffs State Park. As I mentioned earlier, this was once the primary MRT route, but is now an alternate route. Even if you don't plan to take the route, be sure to stop at the interpretive display located at the turn. It contains interesting information on the King and Queen bluff formations, which you can see ahead on US 61.

About 3 miles south of the turn on CR 3 to the Great River Bluffs State Park, you pass the Great River Bluffs State Park Bike Camp. This is a self-service camping area specifically for bicyclists. There are five campsites with tables, a common fire pit, water, a trash can, and a vault toilet. Since this is right on US 61, this is very convenient. It would be nice if there were inexpensive bike campsites all along the MRT.

After the bike camp, the MRT routes you off of US 61 onto a pleasant bike path along the banks of the MR leading into La Crescent. The town of La Crescent received its name from the Kentucky Land Company, which wanted to give a romantic sounding name to attract settlers. La Crescent has the copyrighted title as the "Apple Capital of Minnesota." The bluff orchards of La Crescent offer gourmet apple varieties not found in most other places. The MRT passes an outdoor fruit market on the south end of town. Be sure to pick up several apples.

Just a reminder, the US 14 crossing of the MR to La Crosse, Wisconsin, is a bike-friendly bridge. For those continuing on the Minnesota MRT route, continue out of La Crescent on SH 16, with your handlebar bag full of apples.

A few miles out of town the MRT routes you onto CR 26. Although the shoulder comes and goes on this road, and the traffic travels at high rates of speed, I really enjoyed this final stretch of Minnesota. Practically the entire ride is bordered on one side by wetlands teeming with wildlife. Services on the road are sparse, so carry snacks. There is a convenience store and restaurant in Brownsville, as well as camping at Wildcat Landing, a U.S. Army Corps of Engineers-operated facility located just outside of town.

Hungry cyclists are rewarded at the Iowa state line in New Albin. The town has a restaurant that serves good home-cooked meals.

View of the Mississippi River from Great River Bluffs State Park.

Camping

*John A. Latsch SP
US 61, 3 mile south of
Minneiska, MN
507-643-6849 (Primitive)

*Great River Bluffs
State Park Bike Camp
US 61 3 miles south of turn
to the SP

*Prairie Island CG
1120 Prairie Island Rd
Winona, MN
507-452-4501

Pettibone Rv & CG
33 Park Plaza Dr
La Crosse, WI
800-738-8426
2 miles from La Crescent

Great River Bluffs SP
County Rd 3
Winona, MN
507-643-6849

*Wildcat Landing & CG
11011 Hwy 26
Brownsville, MN
507-482-6250

Lodging

*AmericInn
60 Riverview Dr
Winona, MN
507-457-0249

Carriage House B&B
420 Main Street
Winona, MN
507-452-8256

Alexander Mansion B&B
274 East Broadway St
Winona, MN
507-474-4224

Nichols Inn
1025 Sugar Loaf Rd
Winona, MN
866-642-4667

*Quality Inn
956 Mankato Ave
Winona, MN
507-454-4390

*Dresbach Motel
46937 Riverview Dr
La Crescent, MN
507-643-6120

42

Bike Shops

Adventure Cycle & Ski
178 Center
Winona, MN
507-452-4228

*Kolter Bicycle & Fitness
400 Mankato Ave
Winona, MN
507-452-5665

Bike's Limited
1001 La Crosse St
La Crosse, WI
608-785-2326

Kellogg to Iowa State Line (82 miles)

Miles N/S	Directions	Dist	S	T	Services	Miles S/N
	*Kellogg				R	
0	R at SS onto CR18	0.4	0	M		82
0	L onto CR84	8.4	0	L		82
9	L onto US 61	14.4	8	H	CR	73
	*Minneiska				R	
23	L onto Bridge St	0.6	0	M		59
	*Minnesota City					
24	L onto Wenonah Rd	0.5	0	M		58
24	L onto Harbor Dr/Prairie Island Rd.	5.1	0	L	C	58
29	L at SS onto Riverview Dr	1.5	3	L		53
	*Winona				CGLQR	
31	L onto Levee Park Trail bike path which becomes a sidewalk.	0.6	P	L	LR	51
32	R onto Walnut St (bike path ends)	0.3	0	H		51
32	L onto 5th St	0.9	4	M		50
33	R at SS onto Mankato Ave	1.4	4	H		50
34	S on CR17 at the ramp for SH 43	0.5	0	H		48
35	Veer left onto CR15/Homer Rd	3.3	3	M		48
38	Zag L at SS then immediate R onto US 61/14	12.4	8	H	CQ	44
50	R onto exit for CR 101	0.3	0	M		32
51	L at SS onto CR 101	0.1	0	M		32
51	R at YS onto River St/Riverview Dr (*Dakota)	2.3	0	L		32
53	L at SS onto Riverview Dr	0.4	0	L		29
53	Veer L onto Secluded Rd	0.1	0	L		29
54	Begin bike path	2.2	P	L		29
56	R at SL onto US 14	2.5	5	H		27
	*La Crescent					
58	S at SL onto SH 16	2.6				24
61	Turn left onto CR26	21.4	0	M		21
	*Brownsville				CQR	
82	Iowa state line					0

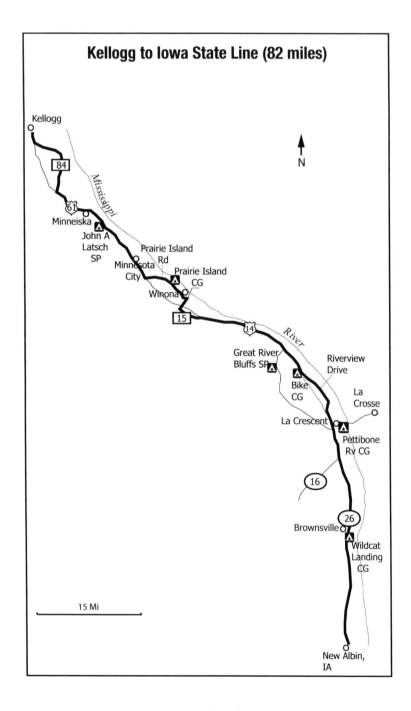

Kellogg to Iowa State Line (82 miles)

Kellogg

N

84

Mississippi

61
Minneiska

John A
Latsch
SP

Prairie Island
Rd
Minnesota
City

Prairie Island
CG

Winona

15

14

River

Great River
Bluffs SP

Riverview
Drive

Bike
CG

La
Crosse

La Crescent

Pettibone
Rv CG

16

26

Brownsville

Wildcat
Landing
CG

15 Mi

New Albin,
IA

Minnesota: Alternate Paul Bunyan Trail
Lake Bemidji State Park to Baxter/Brainerd (108 miles)

The Paul Bunyan Trail is an incredible cycling experience. With over 100 miles of bike paths, connecting the towns of Bemidji and Baxter, the trail provides cyclists a great weekend touring adventure. Currently all but 28 miles of the trail are paved, with another 12 miles from Bemidji to Guthrie scheduled for pavement in the summer of 2008. You may call the Bemidji Tourist Information Center, at 218-444-3541, for an update on the unpaved section.

The PBT passes the shorelines of 21 lakes, routes cyclists through tall pine forests, and crosses bridges over numerous streams and rivers. The grade is basically flat, with much of the route utilizing the abandoned Burlington Northern railway. There are only a few short climbs as the trail passes through the Chippewa National Forest.

The PBT does not follow the MR corridor; therefore, it is not designated as the primary route for the MRT. However, due to this great cycling opportunity, I am including it in the guide as an alternate route. Cyclists could link the PBT with the MRT to create a loop tour of approximately 300 miles.

The northern end of the PBT begins at Lake Bemidji State Park. Shortly after leaving the park, the trail crosses the MR as it leaves Lake Bemidji, offering cyclists a panoramic view of the lake. As it passes through the town of Bemidji, the PBT follows the shoulder on several streets. These streets have painted bike lanes; however, with the wear from highway snow-clearing equipment, the painted lanes have a way of disappearing. After riding these street shoulders for a couple of miles, you reach the beginning of the bike path.

Many of the small towns that once catered to the needs associated with railroads have adapted to accommodating the needs of cyclists. Bikers will have no difficulty obtaining food or lodging. To assist in planning your trip, I have included several of these establishments in the services section, but cyclists will have many more to choose from during the ride.

When you reach the southern end of the PBT in Baxter, you will turn west on Excelsior Road. Follow this road for less than a mile to reach SH 371; then turn south for another $1^1/_2$ miles. The PBT and MRT cross paths at the intersection of SH 371 and College Road.

Camping

Pleasant Pines Resort CG
3443 Pleasant Pine Dr
Hackensack, MN
218-675-6618 (3 miles)

Ruttger Pine Mt Resort
5068 State 87
Backus, MN
218-947-4099

Chlebecek's River RV
3040 16th Ave SW
Pine River, MN
218-587-4112

Lodging

Country Inn & Suites
442 Walker Bay Blvd
Walker, MN
218-574-1400

Pioneer Inn Motel
8098 Hawthorn Trl
Walker, MN
218-547-1366

Bayside Cabins & Bike
206 Rosaland Ave
Backus, MN
218-947-3344

Econo Lodge Hotel
2684 State 371 W
Pine River, MN
218-587-4499

Nisswa Hotel
5370 Merril Ave
Nisswa, MN
218-963-7611

Bike Shops

Trailblazer Bikes
24 Washington St
Brainerd, MN
218-829-8542

Trailblazer Bikes
25336 Smiley Rd
Nisswa, MN
218-963-0699

Back Street Bike Shop
201 5th Street North
Walker, MN
218-547-2500

Lake Bemidji State Park to Baxter/Brainerd (108 miles)

Miles N/S	Directions	Dist	S	T	Services	Miles S/N
0	Lake Bemidji State Park	5.6	P	L	C	108
6	L onto Gould Ave	0.2	4	L		102
6	R onto 1st St (*Bemidji)	0.8	4	M	GLQR	102
7	S at SL onto Shevlin Ave	0.1	4	L		101
7	R onto Clausen Ave	0.6	4	L		101
7	Paul Bunyan Trail	11.6	P	L		101
19	*Guthrie	6.2	P	L		89
25	*Laporte	11.8	P	L	GQR	83
37	*Walker	22.8	P	L	GLQR	71
60	*Hackensack	7.5	P	L	CGLQR	48
67	*Backus	9.3	P	L	CLR	41
77	*Pine River	9.3	P	L	CGLQR	31
86	*Pequot Lakes	6.2	P	L	GLQR	22
92	*Nisswa	15.9	P	L	GLQR	16
108	Baxter				GLQR	0

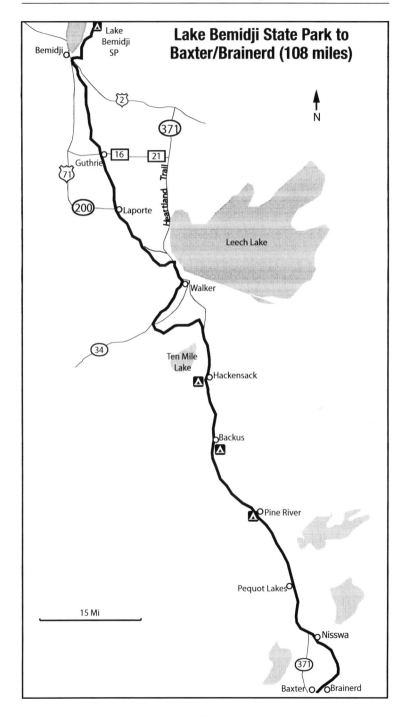

Lake Bemidji State Park to Baxter/Brainerd (108 miles)

WISCONSIN

The Wisconsin segment of the MRT is well equipped to accommodate all types of bicycle touring. With a variety of campgrounds, motels, and bed-and-breakfast establishments liberally dispersed throughout the entire route, cyclists have the flexibility of adjusting their daily itinerary during the ride.

The northern portion of the MRT follows the east bank of the MR, offering great river views and tall sheer bluffs. As you cycle the middle and southern portions, the trail routes you through the rolling farm country for which Wisconsin is known. La Crosse is the only major city the route passes through in the state.

The MRT route in Wisconsin includes riding the Great River Trail. This is a 24-mile-long abandoned railway with a crushed limestone surface. Much of the MRT also overlaps the Great River Road scenic byway.

At this point the MR is now bordered by two states, each with its own MRT. Cyclists now have two options of routes to ride.

As of this publication, the MRT has not been signed in the state of Wisconsin. The trail is 253 miles long in the state.

Wisconsin: Section 1
Prescott to Perrot State Park (92 miles)

The northern end of the Wisconsin MRT is located in the town of Prescott. If you are entering from Minnesota, you will cross the US 61 bridge from Hastings. Shortly after crossing this biker-friendly bridge, you will turn right onto US 10 and follow it into Prescott. The Mileage Log begins in downtown Prescott.

The MRT exits Prescott on SH 35, which you will follow for the next 88 miles. As it leaves Prescott, the MRT passes the Great River Road Visitor and Learning Center. This is a RS. The center not only provides visitors with interesting displays about the area history, it also offers a unique bluff view of the confluence of the St. Croix River and the Mississippi River. From this vantage point you are able to witness the blue water of the St. Croix merging with the brown water of the Mississippi. Initially the water of each river retains its distinctive color. Gradually they merge to produce a motif of blue and brown shades. Finally the sheer volume of the Mississippi River overwhelms that of the St. Croix, and farther downstream you see only the familiar muddy brown water of the Mississippi.

SH 35 provides cyclists with the necessary amenities for an enjoyable ride. The highway has a smooth blacktop surface, with an adequate shoulder, roadside rest stops, and historical markers explaining the history of the area. It follows the high bank of the MR, providing an elevated view across Lake Pepin. There are two Wisconsin State Parks in this section, each right alongside the MRT. The highway also passes through several small towns that provide a selection of eating and lodging establishments.

The first time I rode through this section, there was a sign in the town of Alma that caught my attention. To appreciate the advertisement, you need to know that the town of Alma is located next to Lock and Dam No. 4. The sign for the Pier 4 Café & Smokehouse reads: "The Best BBQ by a Dam Site." I stopped the first time because of the sign; however, I have stopped at the restaurant on each trip since for the barbeque and the open-air dining room overlooking the river.

South of Alma, cyclists have the option of following an alternate course that routes you closer to the MR. See the Mileage Log for details. If you choose not to take the alternate course, continue straight on SH 35. Four miles south of Fountain City, if you wish to leave the Wisconsin MRT and join the Minnesota MRT, the SH 54 bridge will take you to Winona, MN. There is a convenience store on the Wisconsin side of the bridge.

Farther south on SH 35, on the Wisconsin MRT, there is an option for another alternate course. Approximately 4 miles after passing the turn for the SH 54 bridge, watch for the Marshland Access sign. This is a gravel road that routes you through the Trempealeau Wildlife Refuge. The road will emerge from the refuge at the trailhead for the Great River Trail. The primary MRT route continues on SH 35 for another 2 miles before turning onto West Prairie Road, which is a paved route to the Great River Trail trailhead. This is the same trailhead where the alternate route emerges. At this point the MRT follows the Great River Trail as the primary route.

The Great River Trail is approximately 20 miles of converted railway, covered with packed crushed limestone. I rode the trail with full panniers using 700/32-sized tires and did not leave a mark in the trail's surface. The trail routes cyclists through upper Mississippi River Valley prairies and backwaters. This is a great environment for viewing great blue herons, sandhill cranes, egrets, and other waterfowl in their natural habitat. The Great River Trail enters Perrot State Park, which has camping, then continues through the picturesque communities of Trempealeau and Onalaska. Both of these communities offer food and lodging. The Great River Trail requires a $4 pass, which can be purchased at Perrot State Park or at local merchants in Trempealeau and Onalaska. For those cyclists preferring not to ride the Great River Trail, continue on SH 35 where you will rejoin the MRT in the town of Onalaska.

The north entrance to Wisconsin's Great River Trail.

Camping

Lake Pepin CG
1010 Locust Street
Pepin, Wi
715-442-2110

*Merrick State Park
SH 35, 2 miles north
of Fountain City, WI
608-687-4936

*Perrot State Park
1 mile north of
Trempealeau, Wi
608-543-6409

Lodging

River Heights Motel
1020 US 10
Prescott, WI
800-522-9207

*Harrisburg Inn B&B
W3334 Hwy 35
Maiden Rock, WI
715-448-4500

*Pepin Motel & CG
305 Elm Street
Pepin, WI
715-442-2012

*Great River Amish Inn
311 3rd St & Hwy 35
Pepin, WI
715-442-5400

*Fountain Motel
810 South Main Street
Fountain City, WI
608-687-3111

Trempealeau Hotel
150 Main Street
Trempealeau, WI
608-534-6898

Bike Shops

Brone's Bike Shop
615 South Main Street
Fountain City, WI
608-687-8601

Trempealeau Hotel Bike
Rental & Repair
Trempealeau, WI
608-534-6898

Prescott to Perrot State Park (92 miles)

Miles N/S	Directions	Dist	S	T	Services	Miles S/N
	*Prescott					
0	R onto SH 35	19.5	4	M	LGQR	92
20	S at SS on SH 35	4	4	M		73
24	*Bay City	8.2	4	M	R	69
32	*Maiden Rock	6.1	4	M	QR	60
38	*Stockholm	6	4	M	R	54
44	*Pepin	8	4	M	CGLQR	48
52	*Nelson, veer L south of town on SH 35	6.1	4	M	QR	40
58	*Riecks Lake Park	1.6	4	M	C	34
60	*Alma	5.4	4	M	GLR	33
65	*Alternate route, R onto CR OO/R onto Kamrowski Rd/R onto Indian Creek Rd	3.7	0	M		27
69	*Alternate route rejoins SH 35	5.5	4	M		24
74	*Merrick SP	3	4	M		18
77	*Fountain City	9	4	M	LQR	15
86	*Alternate route, R onto Marshland Access	1.9	4	M		6
88	R onto West Prairie Rd	1.2	0	L		4
89	L onto GRT (use fee)	2.9	P	L		3
92	*R to enter Perrot SP (MRT continues straight)					0

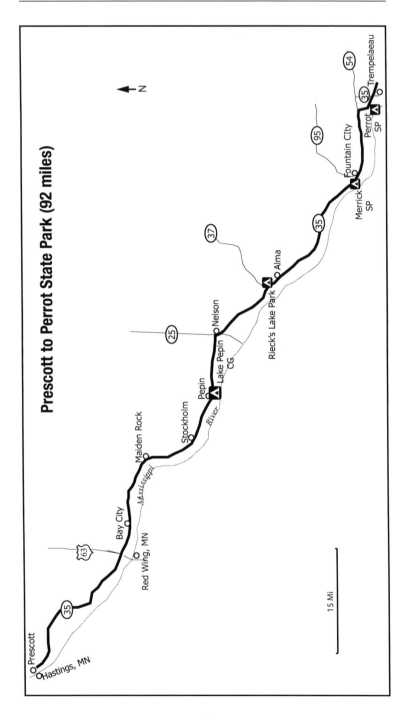

Prescott to Perrot State Park (92 miles)

Wisconsin: Section 2
Perrot State Park to Prairie du Chien (82 miles)

Section one of the MRT ends at the turn for the entrance to Perrot State Park. The MRT continues straight across the entrance, but I recommend entering the park even if you are not intending to camp. The road continues through the park, then routes you into downtown Trempealeau. Treat yourself to lunch or dinner at the Trempealeau Hotel's open-air dining area, overlooking the MR. Exit town on SH 35 to rejoin the MRT on the Great River Trail as it crosses the highway 1 mile south of town.

Once again on the bike path, the MRT takes you deep into the prairie wetlands of the Black River bottoms. Listen for the trumpet-like garoo-oo-a-a-a-a call of the sandhill crane. The path includes several bridge crossings, including a 287-foot-long railroad trestle over the Black River.

As the Great River Trail ends in Onalaska, continue following bike route signs crossing Irving and Hickory streets. The La Crosse area has signed bike routes that generally coincide with the MRT route; however, you should keep the Mileage Log handy because they do differ in areas. Cyclists have a wide selection of eating places at both the north and south ends of the MRT in La Crosse, but not a lot of choices in between.

On an interesting side note: Onalaska was named by the area's first settler/tavern owner, Thomas G. Rowe, after a verse of a poem by Thomas Campbell, "The Pleasures of Hope." The verse was: "And waft across the waves' tumultuous roar / The wolf's long howl from the Oonalaska shore."

The MRT follows the Three Rivers Trail through the La Crosse River marsh. It is good that the community leaders have preserved these natural wetlands for everyone's enjoyment. Within a mile of exiting the bike path, the MRT takes you directly across the campus of the University of Wisconsin-La Crosse. There is not a street sign for the turn onto Badger Street, because the street no longer exists. It has been converted into a pedestrian bikeway. To locate the turn, look for the statue of the eagle at the entrance to the football stadium and then take a right onto the wide walkway that was once Badger Street. You may think that the MRT should have been routed around the campus, but it was pretty cool riding through on my touring bike. Also, if hundreds of touring cyclists were to pass through the campus, it might encourage a few of these young students to consider taking a bike tour of their own, or to at least support cycling in general.

After it leaves the college, the MRT runs through an older neighborhood, with large well-maintained homes, continues through modern neighborhoods, and then reaches the Pammell Creek Bike Trail, before returning to SH 35. If you are in need of supplies at this point, travel north $1/2$ mile on SH 35, where you will find a Wal-Mart®.

Several of the interpretive displays along the MRT attribute the unique topography of southwestern Wisconsin and southeastern Minnesota to the area being a "driftless region." This refers to the area being bypassed by the last ice age, therefore not possessing the silt, clay, sand, and boulders left behind by retreating glaciers, which are common to the other surrounding regions. This also accounts for the tall bluffs and scenic prairie wetlands in this region.

South of La Crosse the MRT continues to follow SH 35, flanked by tall bluffs on one side and the MR on the other. Cyclists ride through several conveniently spaced towns on this stretch. There are a variety of opportunities for a unique dining experience at establishments like the Great River Roadhouse in De Soto, and the Red Lion Pub & Eatery and the Londoners Bistro Pub & Restaurant, both located in Genoa.

Prairie du Chien has an interesting history that can be traced back to the arrival of Jacques Marquette and Louis Joliet in 1673. The famous French explorers, who reached the area by canoe, were the first Europeans to discover a route to the MR. This opened the area to French trappers and a massive French fur-trade industry. This lucrative trade produced Wisconsin's first millionaire. You can learn more about the history of the area by visiting the Fort Crawford Museum, at 717 South Beaumont Road. The museum can be reached by turning left onto Dunn Street for 1 block, then right onto Beaumont Road. You can continue south on Beaumont Road to rejoin the MRT at the corner of Lockwood Street.

Camping

Pettibone RV & CG
333 Park Plaza Drive
La Crosse, WI
608-782-5858

Goose Island CG
W6488 CR GI
Stoddard, WI
608-788-7018
1.8 miles off hwy 35 on
CR GI

Blackhawk Rec Area
County Rd BI
3 miles N of DeSoto, WI
608-648-3314

*Sugar Creek Park CG
Hwy 35
Ferryville, WI
608-734-9406 ($5.00)
(south of town)

Mississippi Bend RV/CG
251 Hillside Drive
Lynxville, WI
608-874-4478

*Big River CG
106 W Paquette Street
Prairie du Chien, Wi
608-326-2712

Lodging

*Onalaska Inn
651 2nd Avenue S
Onalaska, WI
888-359-2619

Maple Grove Motel
5212 Mormon Coulee Road
La Crosse, WI
608-788-0353
(south end of town US 14)

Celtic Inn B&B
924 Cass Street
La Crosse, WI
608-782-7040

*Ellis Safe Landing Motel
329 N Main St
Stoddard, WI
608-457-2122

*Big River Inn
500 Main Street
Genoa, WI
608-689-2652

*Scenic View Cabins
S7602 Hwy 35 B
Desoto, WI
608-648-3329

*Grandview Motel
14812 Hwy 35
Ferryville, WI
608-734-3235

Victorian Rose B&B
225 S. Wacouta Street
Prairie du Chien, WI
608-326-2065

*Super 8 Motel
1930 S Marquette Rd
Prairie du Chien, WI
608-326-8777

Bike Shops

Blue Heron Bicycle
213 Main Street
Onalaska, WI
608-783-7433

Buzz's Bike & Boats
800 Rose Street
La Crosse, Wi
608-785-2737

Smith Cycling & Fitness
125 N 7th Street
La Crosse, WI
608-784-1175

Perrot State Park to Prairie du Chien (82 miles)

Miles N/S	Directions	Dist	S	T	Services	Miles S/N
0	S at SS on GRT at the entrance to Perrot SP	1.8	P	L		82
2	S at SS on GRT	1.1	P	L		80
	*Trempealeau				LR	
3	S at SS on GRT across SH 35	13.7	P	L		79
17	Veer R onto Court St (end of bike trail)	0.5	0	M		66
17	Curve L then R at SS onto 2nd Ave SW then L onto Oak Forest Dr	0.1	0	M		65
17	S at SS on Oak Forest Dr (crossing SH 35)	0.1	0	H		65
	*Onalaska				GLQR	
17	R at SS onto Oak Ave S	1.3	0	M		65
19	L onto Palace St	0.3	0	M		64
19	R at SS onto Larson St, then L on Palace St	0.2	0	M		63
19	Curve R on Rivervalley Dr (bike lane on L)	0.5	P	M		63
20	S at SL onto Rivervalley Dr	0.9	P	M		63
21	L onto Three Rivers Trail (bike path)	1	P	L		62
22	S onto East Ave (bike path ends)	0.6	0	M		61
	*La Crosse				GLQR	
22	R onto Badger St (across from eagle statue)	0.2	P	L		60
22	L on sidewalk across from Whitney Center	0.1	P	L		60
22	S onto 15th St	0.4	0	M		60
23	L at SS onto Cass St	1	0	M		59
24	R onto 29th St	0.3	0	M		58
24	R on Cliffwood Ln 1 block then L on 28th St	0.5	0	M		58
25	L at SS onto Farnam S	0.2	0	M		58
25	R on 31st St	0.2	0	M		57
25	L at YS onto Green Bay St for 1 block then R onto Barnabee Rd	0.2	0	M		57
25	R onto Sunset Dr 1 block then S at SL onto 32nd St	0.9	0	M		57
26	R at SS onto Ward St for a block	0	0	M		56
26	R on 33rd St to begin Pammel Creek bike path on R	1.6	P	L		56
28	R onto US 14/SH 35 then veer right onto SH 35 to exit La Crosse	0.6	4	H		54
28	Veer R onto SH 35	6.3	4	H		54
35	*Stoddard	5.9	2	M	LQR	48
41	*Genoa	10.8	2	M	LQ	42
51	*De Soto	7.8	3	M	CLQR	31
59	*Ferryville	7.5	3	M	GLQR	23
67	*Lynxville	11.4	3	M	C	16
78	R onto CR K/Main St	4.1	2	L	R	4
82	*Prairie du Chien				CGLQR	0

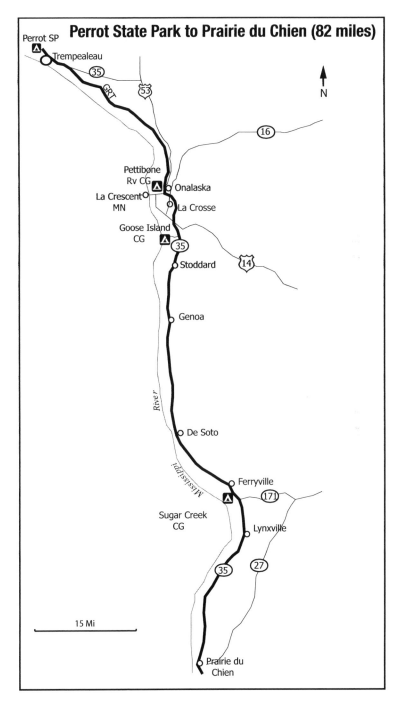

Perrot State Park to Prairie du Chien (82 miles)

Perrot SP
Trempealeau
35
GRT
53

16

N

Pettibone
Rv CG
La Crescent
MN
Onalaska
La Crosse

Goose Island
CG
35

Stoddard
14

Genoa

River

De Soto

Mississippi

Ferryville
171

Sugar Creek
CG
Lynxville

35
27

15 Mi

Prairie du
Chien

Wisconsin: Section 3
Prairie du Chien to Illinois State Line(78 miles)

After leaving Prairie du Chien, say goodbye to SH 35. The MRT has followed the highway through much of our tour of Wisconsin, but at this point it routes cyclists on county roads through rural communities. The roads have no shoulders but the traffic volume is low.

The town of Cassville is an interesting place to stop for a break. This was the hometown of Wisconsin's first governor, Nelson Dewey. The former governor's estate now houses several attractions for area visitors. These include the Nelson Dewey Homesite, largely unchanged from its 1868 construction. Also included on the former estate is the Wisconsin Agricultural Museum, which uses dioramas and exhibits to demonstrate the history of farming in the area. However, the showplace of the estate is The Farmer's Town—30 reconstructed buildings used to replicate a rural community of the early 1900s era. The theme of the area is to tell the intriguing story of how Wisconsin converted a land of forests and prairies into America's Dairyland.

South of Cassville the MRT has something cyclists haven't seen on the route thus far—hills. They're not long steep climbs, but compared to the flat terrain the route has been following, they do get your attention. As you top these knolls, you are rewarded with expansive views of the rolling countryside. You will also see numerous tall grain silos scattered across the landscape.

When you enter the town of Potosi, the MRT continues right on River Lane Road. If you take a side trip to the left, on SH 133, you have the opportunity of riding on the world's longest main street without an adjoining side street. You will also find more services on this road. If you are hungry for catfish, this is the place to be. Potosi lays claim as being "The Catfish Capital of Wisconsin."

The hills become a little steeper, and there are more of them, as these rural roads weave through deep hollows. There are stretches where you can see the MR, but most of the scenery consists of hills and farmland.

The town of Dickeyville has an interesting attraction for visitors—the Holy Ghost Grotto. You may have seen similar folk-art creations like this in your grandparents' early vacation pictures. It is a concrete structure with embedded glass, costume jewelry, shells, and other objects, in the shape of arches, fountains, and a small cave. These formations are built around the Holy Ghost Catholic Church. It was constructed by Father Mathias during the 1920s, when grotto construction was a popular tourist attraction.

The MRT exits Dickeyville on SH 35/US 151. Be sure to watch for the turn off of this highway onto Old Highway Road. There was no sign for the road when I last rode the route. There was a sign for the Wisconsin Woodworks Cabinet at the turn. Also use caution when crossing the four-lane highway for this turn.

When you reach the SH 11 crossing, you are approaching the Wisconsin state border. At this turn you will need to decide if the state on the other side of the border is going to be Illinois or Iowa. Iowa is to the right. Illinois is to the left. The Mileage Log includes directions for each.

For those continuing to Illinois, you have another 5 miles of county roads to ride. About a mile from the Illinois state line you will pass a sight that may seem out of place—a large building complex constructed in the middle of nowhere. This is the Motherhouse of a Catholic religious order for women known as the Sinsinawa Dominican Sisters.

Camping

Wyalusing State Park
13342 CR C
Bagley, WI
608-996-2261

*Nelson Dewey SP
12190 CR V V
Cassville, WI
608-725-5374

Yogi Yellowstone Park
11354 CR X
Bagley, WI
608-996-2201

*Grant River Rec CG
River Lane Road
Potosi, WI
877-444-6777

*Whitetail Bluff CG
8973 Irish Ridge Road
Cassville, WI
608-725-5577

Lodging

Bagley Hotel
175 Bagley Ave
Bagley, WI
608-996-2300

Geiger House
401 Denniston St
Cassville, WI
800-725-5439

*Sandbar Motel
1115 E Bluff St
Cassville, WI
608-725-5300

Plaza Motel
203 S Main St
Dickeyville, Wi
608-568-7562

River View B&B
117 W Front St
Cassville, WI
888-297-5749

Tower Motel
224 Main Street
Dickeyville, WI
608-568-7996

Bike Shops

Prairie Peddler
200 W. Blackhawk Ave
Praire du Chien, WI
608-326-7357

Praire du Chien to Illinois State Line(78 miles)

Miles N/S	Directions	Dist	S	T	Services	Miles S/N
0	*(Prairie du Chien)	1.5	0	M	CGLQR	78
2	L onto Lockwood St	0.3	0	L		77
2	R at SS onto Beaumont Rd	0.2	0	L	C	77
2	Curve L onto Paquette St	0.4	0	L		76
2	L onto Lapointe St	0.4	0	L		76
3	R at SL onto SH 35/US 18	5.2	3	L	GLQR	76
8	R onto CR C	3.1	0	L	C	70
11	R at SS onto CR X	6.9	0	L	C	67
18	S onto CR A	0.1	0	L		60
	*Bagley				CLQR	
18	L at SS onto CR A	4.9	0	L		60
23	R onto CR V v	3.5	0	L		55
27	R at SS onto CR V v	0.7	0	L		52
27	L onto CR V v	8.8	0	L		51
	*Cassville				CGLR	

36	R at SS onto SH 133	4.3	0	M	C	42
40	R onto Far Nuff Rd	0.7	0	L		38
41	L onto Irish Ridge Rd	4.0	0	L		37
45	L at SS onto CR N (street sign missing)	1.0	0	L		33
46	R onto SH 133	6.0	3	M		32
	*Potosi (more town to the left)					
52	R onto River Lane Rd	3.3	0	L	C	26
55	R onto Dean Lane	0.6	0	L		23
56	Curve L onto Ruff Ln	0.4	0	L		23
56	R onto Banfield Rd	1.4	0	L		22
58	Veer L onto Indian Cr Rd (after crossing a bridge)	3.8	0	L		21
62	R at SS onto SH 35/US 61	0.7	0	M		17
	*Dickeyville				GLR	
62	R onto SH 35/US 151	1.0	3	H		16
63	L onto Old Highway Rd (no sign)	1.0	0	L		15
64	R onto CR H	0.5	0	M		14
65	S onto Peddle Hollow Rd	2.3	0	L		14
67	L onto Bluff Rd	3.0	0	L		11
70	L onto Sandy Hook Rd	0.8	0	L		8
71	R onto Badger Rd (cross hwys 35/61/151)	0.7	2	M		8
72	L onto SH 11 (See below for direction to Iowa)	0.8	2	M		7
72	R onto CR Z	2.1	0	L		6
74	R onto Sinsinawa Rd	2.0	0	L		4
76	R at the SS onto Logan Rd/N High Ridge Rd	2				2
78	*Illinois state line					0
	*Alternate route to Iowa					
72	R onto SH 35/ SH 11	0.6				
72	L onto US 61/US 151	1.4				
74	Cross MR into Dubuque, IA					

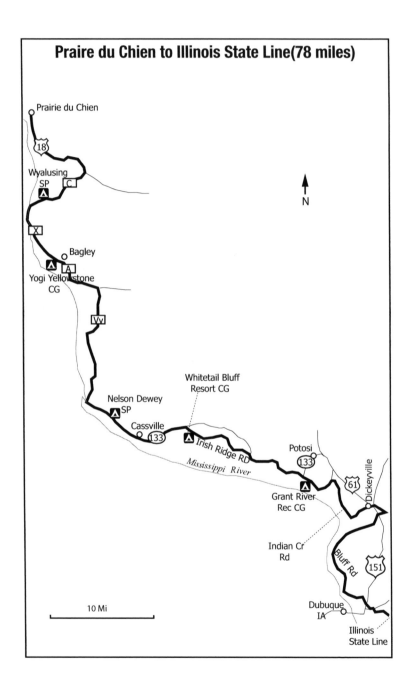

Praire du Chien to Illinois State Line(78 miles)

Prairie du Chien

18

Wyalusing
SP
C

X

Bagley

Yogi Yellowstone
CG

A

W

N

Whitetail Bluff
Resort CG

Nelson Dewey
SP

Cassville

133

Irish Ridge RD

Mississippi River

Potosi

133

Dickeyville

61

Grant River
Rec CG

Indian Cr
Rd

Bluff Rd

151

10 Mi

Dubuque
IA

Illinois
State Line

IOWA

The northern section of the MRT in the state of Iowa routes cyclists over steep hills and wooded terrain. The trail passes many interesting sites, such as Effigy Mounds National Monument, which traces the history of the area's early inhabitants.

As the trail approaches the city of Dubuque, the climbs become less challenging and the forests are replaced by cultivated farmland. This transition from hill country to farm community continues to an even greater extent the farther south you ride.

The towns and parks bordering the MRT in Iowa are conveniently situated so that cyclists should have no difficulty scheduling their eating and overnight stops. With biker-friendly MR bridge crossings in Marquette and Davenport, there are inviting opportunities for multiple day-loop tours into the state of Illinois.

At this time there are individual sections throughout the state with MRT signage. The total mileage of the MRT in Iowa is 318 miles.

W. D. Petersen Memorial Music Pavilion in Davenport, with the Centennial Bridge across the Mississippi River in the background.

Iowa: Section 1
New Albin to Dubuque (85 miles)

The MRT passes through the town of New Albin shortly after it crosses Iowa's northern border. This is a small town, but there is a restaurant and a convenience store.

After riding the flat terrain of the MRT in Minnesota, cyclists are in for a challenging ride across northeastern Iowa's hilly route. These aren't mountains on the scale you encounter in the Western states, but this first section to Dubuque includes several climbs that have an elevation gain of over 400 feet.

In Lansing, take a side trip to 509 Center to see the oldest continuously operated school west of the MR. It is no longer in operation, but the Old Stone School was built in 1863 and operated for 108 years. It is an impressive structure with 2-foot-thick rock walls. Another interesting place to visit in Lansing is the River History Museum, located at 60 South Front Street. The museum has memorabilia and artifacts from the early years of this river community.

Approximately 2 miles north of the town of Marquette, the MRT passes Effigy Mounds National Monument. This is a definite RS. What makes these mounds unique is that they were built in the shapes of birds, turtles, lizards, bison, and bears. Native Americans constructed these mounds 1,400 years ago. They devoted great effort in engineering these burial mounds. Archeologists have unearthed clay in the mounds that is only found on the banks of the river below. This means the builders hauled the clay up this 3,000-foot mountain to where the mounds are located. It is an interesting area and provides an incentive for cyclists to stretch their legs on one or more of the hikes to view the mounds. I recommend the one-hour Fire Point Trail hike. This hike includes many of the major features of the area, plus a great bluff view of the MR.

Leaving Effigy Mounds National Monument, you get a brief break from the hills as you ride through Marquette and McGregor. These are picturesque, small, river communities with several options for lodgings. If you are staying at a commercial lodging, this would be a nice place to stop. Both towns are on the river. In this area you will find a museum, a winery, several bed-and-breakfasts, motels, and also a casino. There will be numerous opportunities to visit an Isle of Capri Casino while riding the MRT. They are positioned along the river all the way to New Orleans. If you would like to visit Prairie du Chien in Wisconsin, there is a biker-friendly bridge across the MR at Marquette.

Pikes Peak State Park is 2 miles south of McGregor. There is a 400-foot climb to its entrance, but the park's hilltop location offers a great view of the river. The park is named after the same famous explorer as the better-known park in Colorado. Several years prior to Zebulon Pike's western adventures, the government commissioned him to explore the MR to select potential military locations to protect the recent Louisiana Purchase acquisition. Pike recommended the strategic position of the park's current location, but the government instead built Fort Shelby on the prairie across the river.

The ride in the Balltown and Sherrill area is very enjoyable. Large portions of this route cross the tops of ridges with great views of the hollows below; also, there is a nice, smooth shoulder to ride on. The tiny town of Balltown is the location of Iowa's oldest operating restaurant. Breitbach's Country Dining originated as a stage coach stop in the 1850s, and is now operated by the sixth generation of Breitbachs. Be sure to stop for a made-from-scratch meal and hear the stories about some of the establishment's famous patrons.

As you enter Dubuque on US 52, the entrance to the Neighborhood Trail is located to your left, immediately after crossing the John Deere Road intersection. Shortly after beginning this trail you encounter an intersection, at which you will turn right. This bike path will route you into downtown Dubuque.

Camping

Red Barn Resort & CG
2609 Hwy 9
888-538-4956
2 miles west of Lansing, IA

*Pikes Peak SP
15316 Great River Road
McGregor, IA
563-873-2341

*Lakeside CG
503 Kosiusko St
Guttenberg, IA
563-252-4151

Finley's Landing Rec CG
Finley Landing Rd
Sherrill, IA
563-552-1571
(3 miles off MRT)

Lodging

McGarrity's Inn
203 Main St
Lansing, IA
866-583-9262

Harpers Café & Motel
415 West Chestnut St
Harpers Ferry, IA
563-586-2403

Eagles Landing B&B
82 North Street
Marquette, IA
563-873-2509

Frontier Motel
101 South 1st St
Marquette, IA
563-873-3497

*Village Motel
821 Walton Ave
McGregor, IA
563-873-2200

*Guttenberg Motel
927 S US 52
Guttenberg, IA
319-252-1433

Bike Shops

N/A

New Albin to Dubuque (85 miles)

Miles N/S	Directions	Dist	S	T	Services	Miles S/N
0	Enter Iowa SR 26 (*New Albin)	11.4			QR	85
11	S onto N 2nd St (*Lansing)	0.3	0	M	GLR	73
12	R onto S Front St/Great River Rd/CR X52	13.8	0	M		73
26	*Harpers Ferry	6.3	0	M	LQR	59
32	L onto SR 76	2.9	0	M		53
35	*Effigy Mounds Natl Monument	4.8	1	M		50
40	Veer R onto Main St (*Marquette-McGregor)	0.7	0	M	GLQR	45
40	L onto CR X56/Great River Rd	6.3	0	M	C	45
47	L onto Marina Rd /3rd St(*Guttenberg)	0.5	0	M	L	38
47	R onto Kosiusko St	0.1	0	M		38
47	L onto N 5th St	0.5	0	M		38
48	R onto Haydn St	0.1	0	M		37
48	L onto US 52	6.6	0	M		37
54	L onto CR C9Y/Great River Rd (*Millville)	7.9	0	L		30
62	* North Buena Vista	4.7	0	L		23
67	S onto Buena Vista Rd	0.8	0	L		18
68	L onto Ridge Rd/CR C63	2	0	L		17
70	S onto Balltown Rd (*Balltown)	6	5	L		15
76	S onto Sherrill Rd/CR C9Y (*Sherrill)	4.8	5	M	R	9
81	L onto US 52 (*Sageville)	2.1	0	H	Q	4
83	L at SL onto Neighborhood Trail	2.1				2
85	*Dubuque				GLQR	0

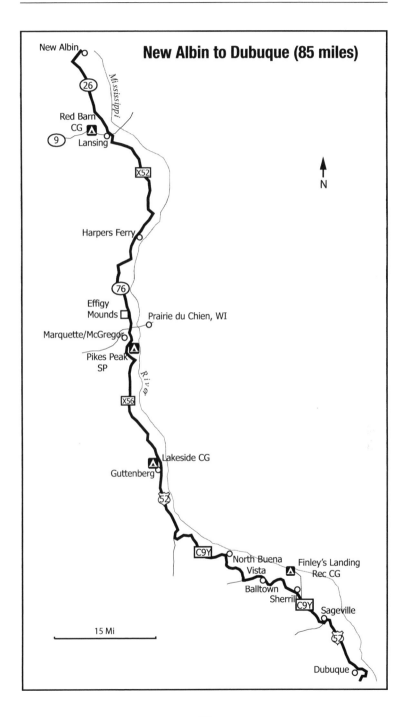

New Albin

New Albin to Dubuque (85 miles)

26

Mississippi

Red Barn
CG
9
Lansing

X52

N

Harpers Ferry

76

Effigy
Mounds
Prairie du Chien, WI
Marquette/McGregor
Pikes Peak
SP

River

X56

Lakeside CG
Guttenberg

52

C9Y
North Buena
Vista
Finley's Landing
Rec CG
Balltown
Sherrill
C9Y
Sageville

15 Mi

52

Dubuque

Iowa: Section 2
Dubuque to Princeton (81 miles)

At the south end of the Neighborhood Trail the MRT follows several urban streets before reaching Dubuque's Main Street. The city has an impressive historic downtown, with Main Street lined on both sides by beautiful brownstone buildings. These well-preserved structures house restaurants, coffee shops, and retail stores, inviting cyclists to take a break. At the south end of Main Street the route follows a pedestrian bridge over a highway, then drops down to Flat Iron Park. If your taste, or budget, runs more in the category of fast food, there is an Arby's® restaurant a block beyond the city park.

Dubuque, considered the "birthplace of Iowa," has several attractions for visitors, such as the National Mississippi River Museum & Aquarium, located in the heart of the Port of Dubuque, at 350 East 3rd Street. Another attraction is the famous Peony Trail, a 2-mile stretch on Grandview Parkway that is lined with those beautiful flowers. To learn more about activities in Dubuque, I suggest visiting the Visitor Center located at the corner of 3rd Street and Main Street.

As the MRT leaves Dubuque it passes through the Mines of Spain Recreation Area. When you reach the intersection of Mar Jo Quarry Road and Monument Drive, before turning down the hill to the right, continue straight to visit Julien Dubuque Monument. Dubuque was the first European to settle in Iowa. When you read about this French-Canadian settler who received a land grant from the Governor of Spain, you begin to understand the history of international involvement for the lands that border the Mississippi River. As the French came down from Canada, the Spanish came up from the south, and both the English and Americans arrived from the east, they all realized the importance of the waterway. Each of these countries claimed ownership of these lands, which resulted in numerous conflicts and political dealings. There were periods in history when settlers along the river were uncertain which country owned the land they were living on.

Back again on the MRT, as you ride through the Mines of Spain Recreation Area you pass interpretive displays about the history of the area. There is evidence of prehistoric Native American cultures living in this area dating back as much as 8,000 years.

There are a couple more climbs between Dubuque and Bellevue. From Bellevue to Princeton, the climbs will be greater in number but will not have the elevation gains of those to the north.

The ride to Princeton includes several unique attractions along the road. It passes through "A little bit of Luxembourg in America," also known as the village of St. Donatus. This small community is striving to preserve the town as a historic Luxembourg village. There is also Sabula, Iowa's only island city. The MRT does not actually pass through Sabula, but cyclists can reach the town with a half-mile side trip. If you do take the detour, be sure to visit the Driftwood Bar & Grill, which has a deck overlooking the MR. A few miles south of Sabula, the MRT passes the site of the Iron Horse Bike and Music Festival. This is not the type of bike you pedal. Warning: traffic could be heavy in this area if your tour coincides with an event at this site.

Located 3 miles north of Clinton is the Bulger's Hollow Recreation Area. At the time I rode through here, the 1-mile detour to the campsite was down a steep gravel road. However, camping was only $4.

The Discovery Trail in Clinton is located to the right of the Cragmor Drive entrance to Eagle Point Park. There is no sign for the trail, which is basically a sidewalk at this end. About a quarter of a mile into the trail, be careful or you might miss the trail's left turn off of this sidewalk. Once again there is no sign for the trail as it makes this turn. The turn is directly across from the street sign for 37th Avenue. The northern half of the Discovery Trail routes cyclists through neighborhoods. The bike path then climbs to the top of the levee, where it offers views of the MR and its bordering wetlands. You also have a view across the MR of an authentic Dutch windmill in Fulton, Illinois. At the southern end of the Discovery Trail you will be at the River View City Park. The park has a campground, and there are a variety of eating establishments a short walk across the railroad tracks.

You are now in the town of Clinton. During the 1880s and 1890s the town was known as the nation's sawmill capital. Logs tied together to form giant rafts, as large as 300 feet wide and 1,600 feet long with crews of thirty men, floated down the MR from Minnesota and Wisconsin during this period. A side tour in the area of 5th, 6th, and 7th avenues will take you past the magnificent homes built by the prosperous sawmill owners. During the peak of Clinton's sawmill industry, the town had more millionaires per capita than any other city in the United States.

When you leave Clinton, you will also leave behind most of the hills on the Iowa portion of the MRT.

Camping

Husemann RV & CG
5447 Olde Massey Rd
Dubuque, IA
563-582-8656
(2 miles off MRT)

South Sabula Lake CG
1516 South Ave
Sabula, IA
563-652-3783
(3 miles off MRT)

*Spruce Creek CG
30711 396th Ave
Bellevue, IA
563-652-3783

Bulger's Hollow Rec CG
Hwy 67
Clinton, IA
563-847-7202
(3 miles north of town)

*Pleasant Creek Rec CG
Hwy 52
Bellevue, IA
309-794-5332
(3 miles south of town)

*River View Park CG
Riverview Drive/9th Ave
Clinton, IA

Lodging

*Richard House
1492 Locust St
Dubuque, IA
563-557-1492

Super 8 Motel
2730 Dodge St (US 20)
Dubuque, IA
563-582-8898

Bounded by Water B&B
601 Pearl St
Sabula, IA
815-541-4919

*Holiday Inn
450 Main Street
Dubuque, IA
563-566-2000

*Gehlen House B&B
101 Main St
St. Donatus, IA
563-773-8200

*Sunset Inn
1111 Comanche Ave
Clinton, IA
563-243-4621

*Julien Inn
200 Main St
Dubuque, IA
563-556-4200

Riverview Hotel
100 S Riverview St
Bellevue, IA
563-872-4142

*Super 8 Motel
1711 Lincoln Way
Clinton, IA
563-242-8870

Bike Shops

Bike Shack Cycling
3250 Dodge St (US 20)
Dubuque, IA
563-582-4381

Backwaters Bike Shop
305 South Second St
Bellevue, IA
563-872-4760

Bicycle World Inc
1072 Central Ave
Dubuque, IA
563-556-6122

Bicycle Station
217 Main St
Clinton, IA
563-242-1712

Free Flight
5010 Wolff Rd
Dubuque, IA
563-582-4500

River City Bike Shop
131 5th Ave
Clinton, IA
563-242-8000

Dubuque to Princeton (81 miles)

Miles N/S	Directions	Dist	S	T	Services	Miles S/N
	*Dubuque				GLQR	
0	S at south end of Neighborhood Trail onto Kniest St (cross Elm St)	0	0	M		81
0	R onto E 21st St	0.1	0	M		81
1	L onto Washington St	0.4	0	M		81
1	R onto 15th St	0.2	0	M		81
2	L onto Main St	1.2	0	M		80
2	S onto Railroad St	0.3	0	M		79
2	L onto Harrison St	0.2	0	M		79
3	L onto Southern Ave	0.7	0	M		79
3	L onto Grandview Ave	0.3	0	M		78
4	R onto Julien Dubuque Dr	0.7	0	M		78
4	R onto Inland Ln	0.1	0	M		77
7	L onto Mar Jo Quarry Rd/Mines of Spain Rd	3.2	0	L		77
8	R onto Old Massey Rd	0.8		L	C	74
14	L onto US 52	36.1	0	M		73
	*St. Donatus		0	M	LQR	67
	*Bellevue		0	M	GLQR	57
45	R onto SR 64/US 67 (*Sabula)	0.5	0	M	CQR	37
58	L onto US 67	12.9	0	M	C	36
58	L onto Cragmor Dr (then immediate R)	0	0	M		23
61	Discovery Recreation Trail	3	P	L		23
61	L onto Riverview Dr (*Clinton)	0.6	0	M	CGLQR	20
62	R onto S 1st St	0.6	0	M		20
62	R onto 7th Ave S	0.1	0	M		19
62	L onto S 2nd St (1 block)	0	0	M		19
62	R onto 8th Ave S	0.1		M		19
62	L onto S 3rd St	0.3	0	M		19
63	S onto 11th Ave S	0.1	0	M		19
65	L onto Comanche Way/Lincoln Way/US 30	2.9	0	M		19
67	L onto US 67/Washington Blvd	1.3	0	H		16
67	S onto Washington Blvd	0.6	0	H		14
68	L onto 4th Ave	0.4	0	M		14
68	R onto 2nd St	0.1	0	M		13
68	L onto 6th Ave	0.05	0	M		13
68	R onto 1st St	0.3	0	M		13
68	R onto 11th Ave	0.1	0	M		13
69	L onto 3rd St	0.7	0	M		13
70	L onto S Washington Blvd	0.8	0	H		12
81	L onto US 67/Great River Rd	11.3	0	M	QR	11
81	L onto Lost Grove Rd (1 block)	0	5	M		0
81	*Princeton				QR	0

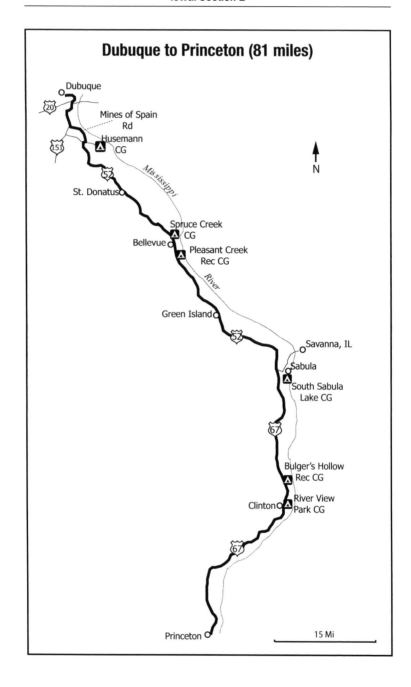

Dubuque to Princeton (81 miles)

Dubuque

20

Mines of Spain
Rd

151

Husemann
CG

52

St. Donatus

Mississippi

N

Spruce Creek
CG

Bellevue

Pleasant Creek
Rec CG

River

Green Island

52

Savanna, IL

Sabula

South Sabula
Lake CG

67

Bulger's Hollow
Rec CG

Clinton

River View
Park CG

67

Princeton

15 Mi

Iowa: Section 3
Princeton to Wapello (72 miles)

The Buffalo Bill Museum is located on Front Street in the town of Le Claire, just off of the MRT. The museum not only features exhibits on the famous Indian scout, but also includes displays on bridge engineer James Buchanan Eads, and other notable people associated with the area's history.

As the MR leaves Le Claire it makes a 90-degree turn to the west, then flows 43 miles to the town of Muscatine before resuming its southern course. Native American legend says the state's northern bluff region was so beautiful that the great river turned back to have a second look before continuing on to the Gulf of Mexico.

The combined communities of Bettendorf and Davenport form the most populated area along the MRT in Iowa. However, as you enter the city of Bettendorf the MRT routes you onto the Riverfront Trail, avoiding the traffic and confusion usually associated with cycling in heavily populated areas. This is an almost 7-mile paved bike/pedestrian path that borders the MR. Thanks to the Davenport political representatives' anti-levee and anti-floodwall policies, the trail runs alongside the banks of the river, allowing cyclists to get closer to it than they have in some time. The philosophy of the area representatives is to: "Let Mother Nature take her course; we'll all be better off."

There are interpretative displays along the Riverfront Trail as well as art exhibits. If your timing is right as you ride the trail, you may be entertained by live music performed at the W. D. Petersen Memorial Music Pavilion. This is a beautiful open-air bandstand constructed in a park on the river bank.

If you would like to cross the MR into Illinois, to visit Moline or Rock Island, the Government Bridge has a separated, protected lane for cyclists. There are signs on this bike trail directing you to the bridge. The Riverfront Trail terminates on the southern end in Credit Island Park. The park is not a part of the MRT route, but it is a nice place to stop for a break.

As I mentioned earlier, the MRT routes cyclists on the outskirts of Davenport; however, it is worth your time to venture off the trail to explore the historic Quad Cities. This area was the location of the first railroad bridge across the MR, referred to by steamboat captains as "The Gate of Death." This is in reference to the famous wreck of the Effie Afton steamboat that crashed into the bridge and its owners consequently sued the railroad company. This came at a period when the railroad industry threatened the riverboats as the preferred means of transporting goods to market. The railroad hired a young, lanky lawyer by the name of Abraham Lincoln to represent it in this publicized trial. In the end the jury decided in favor of the railroad. If you are interested in learning more about attractions in the Quad Cities area, stop at Davenport's historic Union Station Visitor Center, at 102 South Harrison Street. The center is located across the railroad tracks from the Petersen pavilion.

South of Davenport, the MRT diverts away from SH 22 onto lesser-traveled county roads that routes you past Wildcat Den State Park. One of the finest examples of mid-nineteenth century grist mills remaining in the country, the Pine Creek Grist Mill, is located in the park. The park also has a small campground with sites for $6. I passed an interesting roadside memorial in this area. The small memorial erected on private land was for an early settler in Muscatine, who was murdered as the result of a disagreement with a son-in-law. I'm sure there's a story behind this.

The MRT continues south through the town of Muscatine, once known as the "Button Capital of the World". Until I stopped at the Muscatine History & Industry Center, located at 117 West Second Street, I had never heard there had been a button industry on the MR. From the late 1800s to the early 1900s the town of Muscatine had over 45 button factories, producing over 40% of the pearl buttons in the world. The exhibits at the center demonstrate the entire process of harvesting clam shells from the MR to the finished product. This is an interesting stop.

South of Muscatine, the MRT routes you through the "island" of Muscatine. At least, it was an island at one time, before the MR changed its course. Now this fertile farmland is the home of the famous Muscatine melon market.

The remainder of this section follows the Great River Road on county roads through hilly farm country, offering an occasional glimpse of the MR in the distance. When you reach the MRT turn for CR G62, CR X61 does continue straight to link up with SH 99. However, at this time CR X61 includes a section of gravel shortly after the turn; thus the reason for the MRT to use the paved CR G62 to route cyclists to SH 99. This MRT course also takes cyclists to within a short 1-mile side trip to Wapello, which has food and lodging.

Camping

Lakeside RV & CG
11279 140th St
Davenport, IA
563-381-3413

*Buffalo Shores CG
Hwy 22
Buffalo, IA
563-328-3281

*Wildcat Den SP
1884 Wildcat Den Rd
Muscatine, IA
563-263-4337

*Flaming Prairie CG
14624 CR X61
Wapello, IA
319-523-8381
(short gravel entrance)

Snively Access CG
CR X61
Wapello, IA
319-523-8381
(just south of G62 turn)

Lodging

*Holiday Inn Express
1201 Canal Shore Dr
Le Claire, IA
866-270-5110

City Central Motel
1138 State St
Bettendorf, IA
563-355-0268

Fulton's Guest House
1206 E. River Dr
Davenport, IA
800-397-4068
(just off the MRT)

Radisson Quad City Plaza
111 East 2nd St
Davenport, IA
888-201-1718

Super 8 Motel
410 E 65th St
Davenport, IA
563-388-9810

Super 8 Motel
US 61/SH 38
Muscatine, IA
563-263-9100

AmericInn
3115 Hwy 61 N
Muscatine, IA
563-263-0880

Strawberry Farm B&B
3402 Tipton Rd
Muscatine, IA
563-262-8688

Hotel Wapello
227 N Main St
Wapello, IA
319-523-2341

Bike Shops

Healthy Habits Bike Shop
3441 Devils Glen Road
Bettendorf, IA
563-332-5145

Jerry & Sparky's Shop
1819 E Locust St
Davenport, IA
563-324-0270

Trek Bike Store
3616 Eastern Ave
Davenport, IA
563-386-5533

Wolfe's Village Bike Shop
1018 Mound St
Davenport, IA
319-326-4686

Harper's Cycling
1106 Grandview Ave
Muscatine, IA
563-263-9073

Princeton to Wapello (72 miles)

Miles N/S	Directions	Dist	S	T	Services	Miles S/N
	*Princeton					
0	R onto River Dr	0.4	0	M		72
0	R onto Chestnut St (1 block)	0	0	M		72
0	L onto US 67	5.8	0	H		72
	*Le Claire				GLQR	
6	L onto Eagle Ridge Rd/Canal Shore Dr/Sycamore Dr	1.7	0	L		66
8	L onto S Cody Rd/US 67	2.7	2	H		64
11	R onto Spencer Rd (1 block)	0	0	M		62
11	L onto Valley Dr	2.7	1	M		62
13	R onto State St/Hwy 67(*Bettendorf)	2.4	0	H	GQR	59
16	Veer R onto Grant St (one way)	0.6	0	H		56
16	L onto 17th St/George Thuenen Dr	0.3	0	H		56
17	R onto Riverfront Trail (*Davenport)	6.6	P	L	GLQR	56
23	R onto Credit Island Ln (immediate L onto W River Dr/US 61)	0.9	0	H		49
24	L onto Concord St	3.7	0	L		48
28	R onto Utah Ave	0.2	0	M		44
28	L onto Front St/SH 22 (*Buffalo)	10.3	0	M	CQR	44
38	R onto Wildcat Den Rd	0.8	0	L	C	34
39	L onto New Era Rd	2.3	0	L		33
41	R onto Vail Ave	0.2	0	L		31
42	L onto New Era Rd	3.2	0	L		31
45	L onto Sweetland Rd	1.4	2	L		27
46	R onto SH 22	2.2	0	M		26
48	R onto Diagonal Rd/SH 22	0.2	0	M		24
49	R onto Washington St (*Muscatine)	0.3	0	M	GLQR	24
49	L onto Park Ave/SH 38	0.4	0	M		23
49	R onto 2nd St/SH 92	0.6	0	H		23
50	L onto Mulberry Ave/SH 92 (1 block)	0	0	H		22
50	R onto Mississippi Dr/SH 92	1.1	0	H		22
51	L onto Green St/SH 92	0.1	0	H		21
51	R onto Grandview Ave/SH 92	0.4	0	H		21
52	L onto Oregon St/CR X61	0.6	0	M		21
52	R onto Stewart Rd	5.3	0	M		20
57	S onto CR X61/Great River Road	11.3	0	L		15
69	R onto CR G62/CR I Ave	3.4	0	L		3
	*Wapello (R 1 mile off MRT)				GLQR	
72	L onto SH 99					0

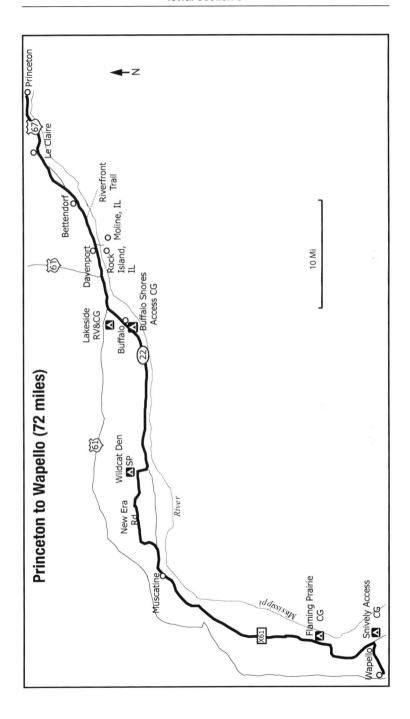

Princeton to Wapello (72 miles)

Princeton

Le Claire

67

Bettendorf

Riverfront Trail

Moline, IL

Davenport

Rock Island, IL

61

Buffalo Shores Access CG

Lakeside RV&CG

Buffalo

22

Wildcat Den SP

61

New Era Rd

River

Muscatine

Mississippi

Flaming Prairie CG

X61

Snively Access CG

Wapello

N

10 Mi

Iowa: Section 4
Wapello to Keokuk (79 miles)

The signing for the highway at the northern end of this section is somewhat confusing. There are signs referring to the road as both CR 99 and CR X99. Iowa maps also show the road as SH 99. This shouldn't be a problem for cyclists; there is only one paved highway to choose from in this area. Just follow highway 99, however it is signed.

Highway 99 cuts through more rolling Iowa farmland. The Hopewellian mounds are located alongside this road at Toolesboro. These are the burial mounds of an ancient culture from the 200 B.C. to 300 A.D. time frame. The summer hours for the museum at the site are Tuesday through Sunday, 12:30 p.m. to 4:30 p.m. Visitors may view the mounds even if the museum is closed.

Shortly after the MRT passes the mounds, it crosses the Iowa River. We have already seen rivers such as the Minnesota, the Crow, the St. Croix, the Wisconsin, the Rock, and the Chippewa feed into the MR, and we are only in the Upper Mississippi River region. The river's largest tributaries are yet to come farther downstream. The Mississippi River has the third-largest drainage basin in the world, with thirty-one states and two Canadian provinces included in its watershed. With this massive accumulation of water, it is difficult to comprehend how man could even begin to manage or contain the mighty river by the time it reaches Louisiana.

Burlington is the first city on this section that offers lodging. There are several bed-and-breakfasts within a few blocks of the MRT; however, cyclists will need to ride 2 miles west to US 61 to locate a motel. The friendly people at the Port of Burlington Welcome Center, located just south of the US 34 bridge, can provide cyclists directions to the lodging. They can also provide information about area attractions to see during your visit. While you are stopped at the visitor center, be sure to pause a moment to admire the US 34 bridge. This impressive structure is a one-tower cable-stayed bridge, connecting Burlington, Iowa, with Gulf Port, Illinois. Cable-stayed bridges are commonly used when the spanned distance is greater than a cantilever bridge can handle and not long enough to justify the more expensive suspension bridge. Watch for examples of all three types of these bridges as you ride the MRT.

South of Burlington you ride through Crapo Park. While in the park, stop to enjoy the view of the MR from the observation overlook. You can also visit the 1909 Hawkeye Log Cabin Museum on display here. The park includes restrooms and picnic facilities.

Campgrounds are at a premium in the northern half of this section. Since 4th Pumping Station campground is 4 miles off of the MRT, all of it on a gravel road, the Spring Lake Campground is very important for cyclists who are camping. There was no sign for the campground when I rode this section; watch for the turn off of Summer Street onto Spring Lake Road, $3^1/_2$ miles south of Crapo Park. The campground is half a mile off of the MRT on this road.

The documented route for the MRT south of Burlington includes 345th Avenue. When I rode through here, 345th Avenue was gravel. In the Mileage Log I included this road; however, I recommend bypassing 345th Avenue until it has been paved. To bypass this gravel section, continue south on US 61, past the turn for SH 16. Continue about another mile, and turn right onto 175th Street/CR J48. After riding less than a mile on this road, you will pass the intersection where you would have come out on 345th Avenue, if you had remained on the MRT. Life is good again now that you are back on the documented route.

Fort Madison would be an ideal place for a scheduled rest day. The area offers lodging, dining, camping, and a variety of attractions. On your day off the bike, you could visit Old Fort Madison to discover military life as it was when this area was still a part of the Louisiana Purchase. In this accurate reconstruction of an 1808 fort, interpreters dressed in period costumes demonstrate the day-to-day tasks of soldiers and their families. You could also visit the North Lee County Historical Museum, listed on the National Register of Historic Places. Another option would be to pick up a tour brochure of the historical area from the Visitor Center, located at 709 9th Street. Or you could just sit on the river bank and watch the river flow past.

After leaving Fort Madison, you ride through the town of Montrose. You may have difficulty following the Mileage Log through here, because several of the streets in town are not signed. If there are still no street signs when you ride through town, I recommend veering left on streets that head in the direction of the MR. This should eventually lead you to CR X28, also called River Road, which is the road the MRT follows out of town. As you ride along River Road, you may be able to see the Nauvoo Temple, across the MR in Illinois.

The ride from Montrose into Keokuk offers some great views of the MR. Initially, River Road takes cyclists along the river's banks, then climbs to the top of a bluff for an even grander view. The route then continues past a row of beautiful homes built on the edge of the bluff.

When the MRT reaches US 136, you may turn left to cross the biker-friendly bridge into Illinois. If you plan to camp at the Hubinger Landing campground, continue across US 136 on 2nd Street, then follow the signs to Victory Park. The small campground is located just upriver from the park.

Camping

4th Pumping Station CG
Pump Station Rd
Burlington, IA
319-753-8260
(4 mile gravel road)

Spring Lake CG
3939 Spring Lake Rd
Burlington, IA
319-752-8691

Duck Haven CG
2748 241st St
Fort Madison, IA
319-372-3221

Hubinger Landing CG
401 Mississippi Dr
Keokuk, IA
319-524-3553

Whispering Pine CG
2505 Hilton Rd
Keokuk, IA
319-524-8403

Lodging

*River's Edge B&B
611 Grand Ave
Keokuk, IA
319-524-1700

Super 8 Motel
3511 Main Street
Keokuk, IA
319-524-3888

*Super 8 Motel
5107 Hwy 61
Fort Madison, IA
319-372-8500

*Santa Fe Motel
2639 Ave L
Fort Madison, IA
319-372-1310

Mississippi Manor B&B
809 4th St
Burlington, IA
319-753-2218
4 blocks off MRT

Super 8 Motel
Hwy 34/Hwy 61
Burlington, IA
319-752-9806

Midtown Motel
2731 Mount Pleasant St
Burlington, IA
319-752-7777

Schramm House B&B
616 Columbia St
Burlington, IA
800-683-7117
(4 blocks off MRT)

Hotel Wapello
227 N Main St
Wapello, IA
319-523-2341

Bike Shops

Bickel's Bicycling
305 E Agency Rd
West Burlington, IA
319-754-4410

Nelson's Bicycle Shop
1214 38th St
Fort Madison, IA
319-372-7528

Wapello to Keokuk (79 miles)

Miles N/S	Directions	Dist	S	T	Services	Miles S/N
	*Wapello (1 mile off MRT to the right)					
0	L onto SH 99/X99	31.7	0	L		79
	*Oakville				Q	47
32	S onto Bluff Rd/Main St (*Burlington)	3.7	0	M	GLQR	47
35	S onto Main Dr/Blackhawk Dr (*Crapo Park)	0.7	0	H		44
36	L onto Madison Ave	1.7	0	M		43
38	Veer L onto CR X62/Summer St	2.5	0	M	C	41
40	L onto Old Hwy 61/120th Ave	2.2	0	M		39
43	L onto US 61	1.6	2	H		37
44	R onto SH 16	1.5	0	M		35
46	L onto 345th Ave	1.3	0	M		33
47	R onto 175th St/CR J48	1.8	0	M		32
49	L onto 330th/CR X38	0.6	0	M		30
49	R onto CR J48/180th St	2.2	0	M		30
52	L onto CR X32/303rd Ave/15th St	4.9	0	M		28
56	R onto Avenue H/US 61 (*Fort Madison)	0.3	0	H	CGLQR	23
57	L onto 18th St/US 61	0.2	0	H		22
57	R onto Avenue L/US 61	10.3	0	M		22
67	L onto SR 998/1st St (*Montrose)	1.1	0	L	QR	12
68	L onto Spruce St (1 block)	0.0	0	L		11
68	R onto Water St	0.2	0	L		11
69	L onto Elm St	0.1	0	L		11
69	R onto Cherry St	0.5	0	L		11
69	S onto Mississippi River Rd/CR X28/River Rd (might be Airport Rd)	9.1	0	L		10
78	R onto Rand Park Ter	0.1	0	L		1
78	L onto Grand Ave	0.8	0	L	L	1
79	L onto Orleans St	0.0	0	L		0
79	R onto 4th St	0.0	0	L		0
79	L onto Franklin St	0.0	0	L		0
79	R onto 3rd St	0.0	0	L		0
79	L onto Fulton St	0.0	0	L		0
79	R onto 2nd St	0.0	0	L		0
	*Keokuk				CGLQR	
79	Cross Mississippi River into Illinois					0

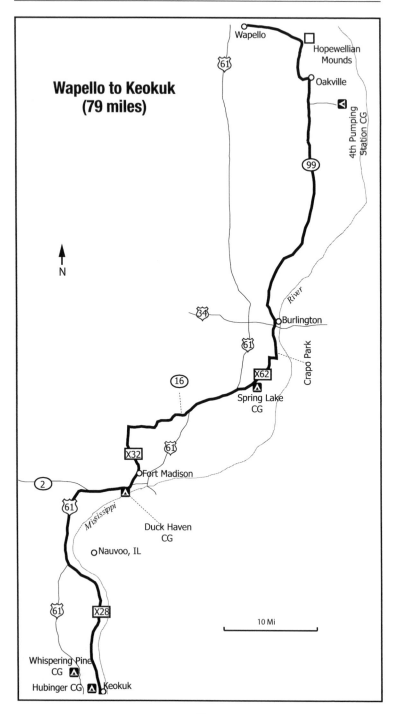

Wapello

Hopewellian
Mounds

61

Oakville

4th Pumping
Station CG

**Wapello to Keokuk
(79 miles)**

99

↑
N

River

34

Burlington

61

Crapo Park

X62

16

Spring Lake
CG

X32

61

Fort Madison

2

61

Mississippi

Duck Haven
CG

Nauvoo, IL

61

X28

10 Mi

Whispering Pine
CG

Hubinger CG   Keokuk

ILLINOIS

MRT, Inc., the League of Illinois Bicyclists, the Illinois Department of Natural Resources, the Bi-State Regional Commission, and the Illinois Department of Transportation all partnered together to create an interesting and enjoyable bicycle route across the state of Illinois. The state's nearly 100 miles of separated bicycle trails gives cyclists a sample of what the MRT will be like when the vision of creating a world-class bicycling route from Itasca State Park in Minnesota to the Gulf of Mexico in Louisiana is realized.

As you ride the MRT across the state, you will pass attractions along the route that trace the rich history of Illinois and the early explorations on the Mississippi River. You will have opportunities to visit museums and interpretative sites constructed at locations where European explorers on the Mississippi River first arrived.

Whether you are camping or staying in commercial lodging, there is no section of the MRT in Illinois where accommodations are not within a reasonable day's ride. Illinois has more MRT miles—584 miles—than any other state on the route. Currently the MRT route in Illinois is not signed.

Authentic Dutch windmill located on the banks of the Mississippi River, in Fulton, Illinois.

Illinois: Section 1
Wisconsin State Line to Port Byron (84 miles)

The vision of the MRT as an uninterrupted off-road trail along the corridor of the Mississippi River is closer to being a reality in the first two sections of Illinois than in any other area along the entire MRT. I personally want to thank those who worked to create the Great River Trail, which is utilized by the MRT in this section.

The entry into the state of Illinois from Wisconsin is without fanfare. There isn't even a state border sign, so you are unsure of the exact point where you enter Illinois. What you are greeted by, however, are unobstructed hilltop views of beautiful farmland. On the clear day I rode this stretch, the view seemed endless. As I paused to enjoy the scenery from the top of one of these knolls, I counted six tall grain silos scattered across the countryside. It turned out to be quite a memorable welcome into the state of Illinois.

The enjoyable ride across these rolling hills takes you to Galena, one of the jewels of the MRT. What a beautiful and interesting village this is. The MRT routes cyclists directly through the historic downtown on Main Street. Main Street is a one-way road, so cyclists coming from the north will need to zag right one block onto Bench Street; but be sure to ride back up Main Street. This is one of the best preserved downtown districts on the MRT. Unlike many historic cities, Galena's downtown is alive with shops, restaurants, and entertainment spots. After visiting the business district, you can cross the Galena River to relax under a tree at the park on the river's banks.

The attractions do not stop in downtown Galena. There are museums and historical sites throughout the area documenting the village's rich history—from the early Native American inhabitants, through the French settlers in the late 17th century, to the migration of American settlers in the early 19th century. Plan for an overnight stay in one of Galena's more than fifty beautiful bed-and-breakfasts. For those camping, Palace Campgrounds, located 2 miles north of town, are the oldest campgrounds in Illinois. The campgrounds also offer cabins at a reasonable rate. For more information on area attractions, stop at the Old Train Depot Visitor Information Center, at 101 Bouthillier Street, 877-444-5850, located to the left just after crossing the US 20 bridge over the Galena River.

As you leave Galena, the intersection of Rives Street and Blackjack Road can be confusing. Rives Street comes to a stop sign, for what should be Blackjack Road, but there is no street sign. Also, after turning right at the stop sign the first mailbox has a Rives Street address. I don't understand why Blackjack Road does not originate at the stop sign, but go ahead and turn right at the stop sign. Within a mile the mailboxes will have a Blackjack Road address. Shortly after leaving Galena, the MRT routes you up a pretty good climb with a 400-foot elevation gain. This is the last climb in this section.

At the south end of the town of Savanna, watch for the right turn to the Chamber of Commerce, housed in a converted railroad car. This turn will take you to the entrance of the Great River Trail. The GRT is an Illinois bike route composed of separated bike lanes and low-traffic roads. You follow the GRT for the next 60 miles to Rock Island.

This first segment of the GRT routes cyclists on a paved trail through MR wetlands. There are pull outs along the path for wildlife viewing. Currently the GRT includes a short ride on SH 84 to reach Riverview Road. There are plans to avoid the highway by using an abandoned railway, which riders will follow directly to Riverview Road.

As you follow the MRT along Riverview Road, be sure to visit the Ingersoll Wetlands Learning Center. This center was established to promote environmental education and the conservation of the MR and its tributaries. The facility is packed with hands-on exhibits that make for a fun learning experience. The center also has an observation area, with binoculars, for viewing wildlife in the surrounding wetlands.

Outside the town of Thomson, just as Main Street makes a sharp left turn, the MRT follows a short path to the right, taking you to an unnamed paved road. Turn right when you reach this road for camping at the Thomson Causeway Recreation Area, or turn left to continue on the MRT. After a short distance you will turn off of the road onto a pea-gravel bike path. This path routes you through a sand prairie wildlife refuge, offering unique opportunities for viewing waterfowl in their natural wetlands environment. Even though this is a gravel path, I had no problems riding it with 700/32 size tires.

In the town of Fulton, the MRT makes a right turn onto 9th Avenue, while the GRT continues straight. The MRT routes cyclists to the Levee Path. The Levee Path not only provides a magnificent view of the river, but it also runs past an authentic Dutch windmill. The windmill was manufactured and pre-assembled in the Netherlands, then re-assembled and installed by Dutch craftsmen at the present location. Situated on the banks of the mighty MR, the 100-foot-tall structure is an uncommon sight.

The MRT route crosses SH 84 to follow lesser traveled side roads into the town of Albany. You will exit the town by way of the Albany Mounds State Historic Site. The MRT passes by the burial mounds and interpretative displays on the history of the site. There are restrooms located at the entrance to the historic site.

Shortly after exiting Albany Mounds, the MRT once again crosses SH 84, and then routes you 35 miles on a paved separate bike path. There are sections of the bike path that utilize local streets; however, there are bike route signs through most of this. If you do encounter questionable turns, refer to the Mileage Log. Be sure to read about the interesting history of the area at the kiosk stations along the ride.

Camping

Palace CG & Cabins	*Palisades State Park	*Fin An Feather CG
11357 US Hwy 20	16327 Hwy 84	6284 Riverview Rd
West Galena, IL	Savanna, IL	Thomson, IL
815-777-2466	815-273-2731	815-273-3302
*Thomson Causeway	Lock & Dam 13 CG	Camp Hauberg
Lewis Ave	North of Fulton, Hwy 84	12928 Hwy 84 V
Thomson, IL	Primitive Camping	Port Byron, IL
815-259-3628		309-523-2168

Lodging

Best Western Suites	Ramada Inn	Hellman Guest House
9923 W US 20	11383 W US 20	318 Hill St
Galena, IL	Galena, IL	Galena, IL
877-722-2577	815-777-2043	815-777-3638
Grandview Guest House	Super 8 Motel	Thomson House Lodge
113 S Prospect St	101 Valley View Dr	800 One Mile Road
Galena, IL	Savanna, IL	Thomson, IL
815-777-1387	815-273-2288	815-259-7378
Pine Motel	*Leisure Harbor Inn B&B	Olde Brick House B&B
19020 13th St	701 Main Ave	502 N High St
Fulton, IL	Cordova, IL	Port Byron, IL
815-589-4847	309-654-2233	309-523-3236

Bike Shops

Arnold's Bike Shop	Bicycle Station	River City Bike Shop
831 Main Street	217 Main St	131 5th Ave S
Thomson, IL	Clinton, IA	Clinton, IA
815-259-8289	563-242-1712	563-242-8000

Wisconsin State Line to Port Byron (84 miles)

Miles N/S	Directions	Dist	S	T	Services	Miles S/N
0	Enter Illinois on Logan Rd/High Ridge Rd	6.2	0	L		84
6	L at SS onto SH 84	0.8	0	M		78
7	R at SS onto Council Hill Rd/CR 1	1.5	0	L		77
9	R onto N Council Hill Rd/CR 2	2.3	0	M		75
11	S onto Dewey Ave/Broadway St/Main St (*Galena)	1.1	0	H	CGLQR	73
12	L at SL onto US 20 (bike path on north side of bridge)	0.2	0	H		72
12	R onto 3rd St	0.2	0	M		72
12	L onto Rives St	0.1	0	M		72
12	R onto Blackjack Rd/CR8	14.6	0	L		72
27	R at SS onto SH 84 (*Hanover)	14.6	0	M	GLR	57
	*Palisades SP					
	*Savanna				GLQR	
42	Great River Trail (GRT)	3.2	P	L		42
45	R at SS onto SH 84	1.4	0	M		39
46	R onto Riverview Rd	4.5	0	L		38
51	L onto Sandpatch Rd	0.5	0	L		33
51	R onto Sandridge Rd	1	0	L		33
52	Veer L onto Main St (*Thomson)	0.1	0	L	CGLQR	32
52	R onto GRT	7	P	L		32
59	R onto 9th Ave (*Fulton)	1.1	0	L	CGLQR	25
60	R onto 2nd St	0	0	L		24
60	L onto Levee path	0.3	P	L		24
61	Veer L then R onto GRT bike path	1.9	P	L		23
63	R onto 4th Ave to cross RR tracks and follow signs to levee path	0.3	0	L		21
63	R onto Ward Rd	0.2				21
63	L onto Diamond	0.1	0	L		21
63	R to Cattail Slough then L onto Levee Path	0.9	P	L		21
64	R onto Ebson Rd	1.3	0	L		20
65	L onto Garden Plain Rd (Cross SH 84)	0.1	0	L		19
66	R onto Kennedy Rd	0.4	0	L		18
66	R onto Ufkin Rd (packed gravel)	0.5	0	L		18
66	R at SS onto Palmer Rd	0.8	0	L		18
67	L at SS onto Waller Rd/Bluff St (*Albany)	1	0	L	QR	17
68	R at SS onto 1st St Ave then left onto Church St	0.2	0	L		16
68	L onto 11th Ave	0.6	0	L		16
69	R at YS to Albany Mounds Historic Site	1	P	L		15
70	R onto Bunker Hill Rd then R at SS onto Meridosia Rd	0.3	0	L		14
70	At SS cross SH 84 then L onto GRT	4.6	P	L		14

75	R at nuclear plant exit	0.1	P	L		9
75	L onto bike path	1.1	P	L		9
76	L at SS then immediate R to bike path.	1.7	P	L		8
78	R onto 171st Ave then L onto River Rd (*Cordova)	0.7	P	L	R	6
79	R onto 3rd Ave then L onto 9th St	0.4	P	L		5
79	R at SS onto Main Ave	0.2	P	L		5
79	L onto 6th St	0.1	P	L		5
79	R at SS onto 3rd Ave	0.1	P	L		5
79	L at SS onto 4th St	0.4	P	L		5
80	Curve onto 10th Ave then L onto 3rd St	0.3	P	L		4
80	L onto 13th Ave then R onto bike path	3.9	P	L		4
84	(*Port Byron)				CLQR	0

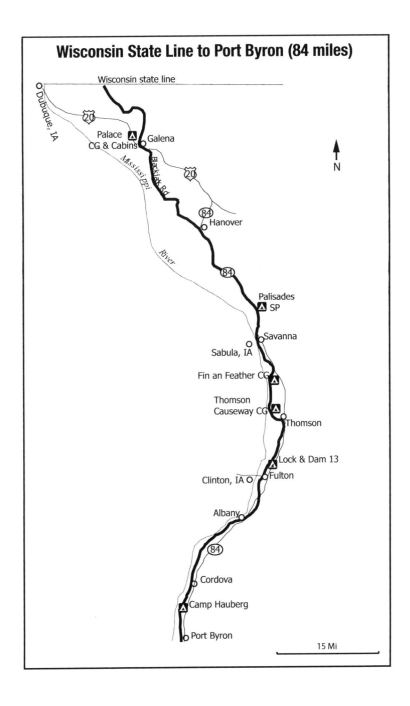

Wisconsin State Line to Port Byron (84 miles)

Wisconsin state line

Dubuque, IA

Palace CG & Cabins

Galena

Mississippi

Blackjack Rd

River

Hanover

Palisades SP

Savanna

Sabula, IA

Fin an Feather CG

Thomson Causeway CG

Thomson

Lock & Dam 13

Clinton, IA

Fulton

Albany

Cordova

Camp Hauberg

Port Byron

N

15 Mi

Illinois: Section 2
Port Byron to Oquawka (89 miles)

The separated bike path continues through Port Byron, alternating between running alongside the shoulder of SH 84 and the banks of the MR. The segments of the MRT that run along the river pass interpretative displays and roadside parks. Stop for a break at one of these parks to watch the river flow past. Or even better, stop for ice cream in Hampton's restored riverfront district, then enjoy your treat as you sit on the river bank. I watched an entire mature tree float past in the swirling river current. The MRT passes two campgrounds in the Hampton area.

In Moline and Rock Island the bike path runs along the top of the levee, providing sweeping views across the river to its Iowa shores. If you are seeking lodging, you won't find anything in the area more conveniently located than Stoney Creek Inn. The bike path actually curves around the hotel. When the trail reaches Jumer's Casino & Hotel, you can take one of the streets to the left to reach Rock Island's Art and Entertainment District. For more information on the area, stop as the MRT passes by the Quad Cities Convention and Visitors Bureau, 1601 River Drive, Suite 110, 800-747-7800.

There is a sign on the MRT in Rock Island for Government Bridge, a biker-friendly crossing to Davenport, Iowa. This bridge also passes Rock Island Arsenal, the nation's largest government owned and operated arsenal. In 1809 an act of Congress set the island aside as a federal military reservation. There is a museum with displays and artifacts on the history of Arsenal Island, as well as exhibits on the history of small-arms development. The museum is open to the public, Tuesday through Sunday from 8 a.m. to 4 p.m.

The separated bike path ends when you exit Sunset Marina Park. Once back in the real world, where you share the road with vehicles that are much larger than your bicycle, you cross a bridge over the Hennepin Canal. This canal has an interesting history. As early as 1834 Illinois statesmen were discussing construction of a canal to link the Illinois River with the Mississippi River, and shorten the route between Chicago and Rock Island by over 400 miles. The canal was delayed for financial reasons until 1892, when Congress authorized construction to begin. The first boat passed through the canal in 1907. However, during the years the canal was being built, the U.S. Corps of Engineers widened the locks on both the Illinois and Mississippi rivers. Even before a boat made the maiden run on the Hennepin Canal it was already obsolete, because the canal could not accommodate the larger vessels being used.

There are several camping options during the next 50 miles, but they are not directly on the MRT. To reach the Rock Island KOA, at the turn for Ridgewood Road, continue on 78th Avenue another $1/2$ mile and you will reach the campground. Near Taylor Ridge, there is a sign for Hidden Lake Campground on SH 192. After making this turn onto 123rd Street, it is about 1 mile to the campground. The road is paved to the campground's entrance. Loud Thunder Forest Preserve is located another 2 miles past the turn off of SH 192 onto SH 92. Rather than make this left turn, continue straight on SH 92 to the park entrance. The nearest camping in the preserve, Silva Campground, is about another mile on paved road after entering the park. To reach camping in the town of Keithsburg, at the turn onto Main Street, continue straight another 2 blocks on 4th Street.

After leaving Rock Island the terrain is flat and open. There are no shoulders on the roads, but visibility is good for motorists to see a cyclist. The roads in this area are not well signed. If in doubt about the name of a highway, watch for addresses on mailboxes and follow signs that direct you to towns that the MRT passes through. As the route takes you through the Big River State Forest there is a change of scenery, with dense woods bordering the roadsides. All three of the campgrounds along this stretch are nestled among tall pine trees and provide an inviting setting. There is no street sign for 3rd Street as you approach the town of Oquawka. Follow the sign off of CR 3 for Delabar State Park. At the entrance for the park, continue left to reach town.

Camping

Fisherman's Corner CG
16123 Hwy 84 N
Hampton, IL
309-794-4524
(1/2 mile north of town)

*Illiniwek Forest CG
Hwy 84
Hampton, IL
309-496-2620

Rock Island KOA
2311 78th Ave W
Rock Island, IL
309-787-0665

Hidden Lake CG
11827 120th Ave W
Taylor Ridge, IL
309-795-1138

Loud Thunder Preserve
19408 Loud Thunder Rd
Illinois City, IL
309-795-1040

Keithsburg Riverside CG
400 S 3rd St
Keithsburg, IL
309-374-2311
(2 block off MRT)

*Riverview CG
Keithsburg Rd
Keithsburg, IL
309-374-2496

*Shady Pines CG
Keithsburg Rd
Keithsburg, IL
309-374-2496

*Delabar SP
3rd St
Oquawka, IL
309-374-2496
(1 mile north of town)

Lodging

*RiverEdge B&B
4234 River Drive
Moline, IL
309-797-6442

*Stoney Creek Inn
101 18th St
Moline, IL
309-743-0101

American Motor Inn
4300 11th St
Rock Island, IL
309-788-7673

*Hillside Inn
4715 11th St
Rock Island, IL
309-788-0612

Top O' Morning B&B
1505 19th Ave
Rock Island, IL
309-786-3513

Milan Motel
103 2nd Ave E
Milan, IL
309-787-1711

Keithsburg Motel
200 Main St
Keithsburg, IL
309-374-2659

Pine View Cabins
Oqauwka, IL
309-587-3217
(2 miles north of town)

River Bed Inn
E Hwy 164
Oquawka, IL
309-876-4321

Bike Shops

Bike N Hike
3913 14th Ave
Rock Island, IL
309-788-2092

Jerry & Sparky's Shop
1819 E Locust St
Davenport, IA
563-324-0270

Harper's Cycling
1106 Grandview Ave
Muscatine, IA
563-263-4043

Port Byron to Oquawka (89 miles)

Miles N/S	Directions	Dist	S	T	Services	Miles S/N
	*Port Byron				CLQR	
0	S onto Main St	0.6	P	L		89
1	R onto Walnut St to bike path	0.3	P	L		89
1	R at SS onto Main St	0.5	P	L		89
1	Curve L then R onto bike path	1.3	P	L		88
3	L at SS onto12th St to bike path (*Rapids City)	2.9	P	L	QR	87
6	R as bike path heads to river	0.8	P	L		84
6	R onto 9th St then onto bike path	0.4	P	L		83
7	L at YS onto 1st Ave (*Hampton)	1.1	P	L	C	83
8	L to bike path paralleling hwy	3.5	P	L		82
11	R at SS to follow bike path	2.4	P	L		78
14	L at SS onto 2nd Ave (*Moline)	1.4	P	L	GLQR	76
15	R at SS toward river (*Rock Island)	4.5	P	L	GLQR	74
	*Sign for Government Bridge		P	L		70
20	L then R onto bike path entering Sunset Marina Park.	0.7	P	L		70
20	L onto 31st Ave	1.1	0	L		69
22	R onto 9th St	1.1	0	H		68
23	R at SL onto US 67	1.2	4	H		67
24	R onto 4th St (*Milan)	0.7	0	M		66
25	R onto Andalusia Rd/10th St/78th Ave	0.7	0	M	C	65
25	L onto 14th St/Ridgewood Rd	1.2	0	M		64
26	S at SS onto Ridgewood Rd/CR K	2.6	0	M		63
29	R onto 127th Ave/SH 192	11.6	0	M	C	60
	*Edgington					49
41	L onto SH 92	10.5	0	M		49
	*Illinois City					38
51	L onto CR A/45th St/CR 14	16.3	0	M		38
67	L onto SH 17	2.4	0	M		22
70	R onto 76th St/4th St	6	0	M		20
76	L at SS onto Main St (*Keithsburg)	0.5	0	M	CLQR	14
76	R onto 10th St/CR 25/Keithsburg Rd/CR 3	9.9	0	M		13
	*Riverview CG/Shady Pines CG		0	L	C	3
86	R onto 2225N (no sign)	0.5				3
	*Delabar SP				C	3
87	L onto 3rd St (no street sign)	2.3	0	L		3
89	L onto Schuyler	0.4	0	L	GR	0
89	*Oquawka					0

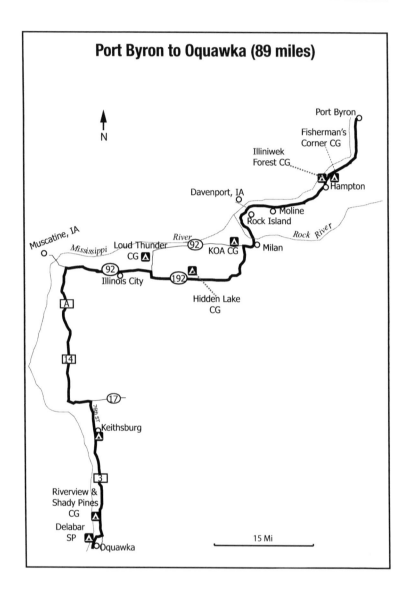

Port Byron to Oquawka (89 miles)

N

Port Byron

Fisherman's Corner CG

Illiniwek Forest CG

Hampton

Davenport, IA

Moline

Rock Island

Muscatine, IA

Mississippi River

Loud Thunder CG

92

KOA CG

Milan

Rock River

92

Illinois City

192

Hidden Lake CG

A

14

17

76th ST

Keithsburg

3

Riverview & Shady Pines CG

Delabar SP

Oquawka

15 Mi

Illinois: Section 3
Oquawka to Ursa (89 miles)

Before leaving Oquawka, take a few minutes to visit some of the historic sites in the village. One of these is the 1887 Civil War monument in remembrance of 200 soldiers who were killed in the Civil War. The cemetery, which adjoins the 1855 historic South Henderson Church, also contains the remains of two Revolutionary War and 29 Civil War veterans. Oquawka is also the gravesite of Norma Jean, the circus elephant. The home of prominent former community leader Alexis Phelps has also been restored. Both Abraham Lincoln and Stephen A. Douglas were rumored to have spent the night in the house. I don't believe the two stayed at the house on the same occasion; Douglas was the Democratic opponent Lincoln defeated for the presidency. Stop by the Oquawka Museum to learn more about the interesting stories behind the village's history.

Three miles south of Oquawka the MRT passes Henderson County Covered Bridge. The bridge was washed away by flooding in 1982. Fortunately it has been restored, and during the process many preparations were taken to keep the structure historically accurate. Seventy-five percent of the bridge's original wood was salvaged from the wreckage. There is also an interesting sign from the bridge's early years, with rules on use of the bridge. The site has restrooms and a picnic area. This is a RS.

Henderson County Covered Bridge, located south of Oquawka, Illinois.

This is a difficult area to document the route through. There doesn't seem to be a common name for some roads that the map indicates as being the same road. A road that appears to be one continuous road has a different name for each end. Also, when a side road joins the main road there is a different name for the main road on each street sign. That is why the Mileage Log has multiple names for some entries. I tried to document the name for both the beginning and ending of a road. This is mainly for the south-to-north cyclists. However, other than the issue with the road signs this is an enjoyable ride through wide-open farm country.

In Dallas City the MRT takes you right along the river's edge at almost river level. Actually, when I rode through, it was below river level. I had to alter my course because of flooding. However, under normal conditions the MRT passes a community park with a restroom and a picnic area. The Riverview Campground is also in the area.

Within 3 miles after leaving Dallas City, SH 9 makes a left turn and the MRT continues straight on highway 1800 E. There is no sign for 1800 E as it leaves SH 9; however, shortly afterwards you will pass a sign on the highway.

The MRT passes through the town of Nauvoo, Hebrew for "peaceful place." Based on my experience when I rode through, the town is appropriately named. I would also use it to describe the residents. They were very patient in answering my questions about the area, and pleasant to visit with.

Nauvoo was founded by Joseph Smith and fellow members of the Church of Christ of Latter Day Saints. It is an interesting story of how these church members were forced to leave the state of Missouri by that state's governor. It is also a very controversial story. If you would like to learn more, stop in one of the village bookstores and I'm sure you will be able to find something on the subject.

There are numerous attractions in Nauvoo: Nauvoo Temple, Illinois' oldest winery, the Monument to Women, the restored historic district, Joseph Smith Homestead, Brigham Young Home, Scovil Bakery—to sample a tasty gingerbread cookie—and many more. To help you plan your visit, stop at one of several visitor centers throughout the village.

Leaving Nauvoo, there is a 3-foot shoulder on the riverside of the road. The shoulder on the off-riverside comes and goes. This is an enjoyable stretch of road, with views of the river and rest stops alongside the highway. In the town of Hamilton, the US 136 bridge provides a biker-friendly MR crossing for those who want to enter Iowa.

After leaving the town of Warsaw you ride one of the stretches I mentioned where the highway name keeps changing. My maps show this 20-mile segment as CR 12 and CR 7, but I didn't see a county road sign on the entire road. Just follow the distances in the Mileage Log and you'll be alright. As an indicator that you are on the right road, about 13 miles south of Warsaw, you should pass a turn to Lima. This turn to Lima is not the MRT route.

The ride through this segment reminded me of summers when I was a carefree kid riding my bike on tractor paths through the fields where I was raised. Even though I was on a paved road through here, I still experienced that same peaceful solitude while riding through the middle of these fields.

Camping

Henderson Co CG
Gladstone Lake RD
Gladstone, IL
309-374-2496
(1 mile off CR 15)

Nauvoo RV CG
2205 Mulholland St
Nauvoo, IL
217-453-2253

*Riverview Cabins & CG
971 W 1st St
Dallas City, IL
217-852-6662

Wildcat Springs CG
840 North 7th St
Hamilton, IL
217-847-2906

*Nauvoo SP
Hwy 96
Nauvoo, IL
217-453-2512

Water Street Park
Downtown
Warsaw, IL

Lodging

New Elms Motel
RR 1
Dallas City, IL
217-852-3829

*Hotel Nauvoo
1290 Mulholland St
Nauvoo, IL
217-453-2211

1850s Guest House
1550 E Hwy 9
Dallas City, IL
217-852-3652

States Motel
1430 Keokuk St
Hamilton, IL
217-847-3338

Nauvoo Log Cabins
65 N Winchester St
Nauvoo, IL
217-453-9000

Retreat House Lodge
RR 2
Ursa, IL
217-964-2243
(side trip off the MRT)

Bike Shops

Bickel's Bicycling
305 E Agency Rd
West Burlington, IA
319-754-4410

Nelson's Bicycle Shop
1214 38th St
Fort Madison, IA
319-372-7528

Oquawka to Ursa (89 miles)

Miles N/S	Directions	Dist	S	T	Services	Miles S/N
	*Oquawka				GR	
0	L onto Schuyler	0.4	0	L		89
0	R onto 8th St/SH 164	4.9	0	M		89
	*Henderson Covered Bridge					
5	R CR15/1600N, follow signs to Lock & Dam 18 (*Gladstone)	3.1	0	M	C	84
8	L onto 900E/CR 15	3	0	L		81
11	R onto 1300N/850E	1	0	L		78
12	R onto US 34	0.5	0	M		77
13	L onto 800E/1170N	0.9	0	M		76
14	R onto 825E	0.7	0	M		75
15	L onto 1100N/825E	0.5	0	M		74
15	R onto 870E/800E	2.1	0	M		74
17	R onto 900N	0.5	0	M		72
18	L onto 750E	1.5	0	M		71
19	L onto 750N	0.5	0	M		70
20	R onto 800E	1.8	0	L		69
21	R onto 575N	2.2	0	L		68
24	L onto 775E/750E	0.7	0	L		65
24	R onto 300N	1.2	0	M		65
26	Curve L onto SH 96 (*Lomax)	4.5	1	M	QR	63
30	R onto 1st Street (*Dallas City)	1.3	0	M	CLQR	59
31	L onto Oak St	0.4	0	M		58
32	S onto SH 9	2.7	0	M		57
34	S onto 1800 E(no sign)	1.1	0	L		55
36	R onto N2600	0.5	0	L		53
36	L onto 1760E/1750E (*Colusa)	1	0	L		53
37	R at YS onto 2500N/CR 2	7.8	0	L		52
45	S onto 2450N	2.1				44
47	L at SS onto 800E	0.5	0	L		42
47	R onto 2400N/SH 96	1.1	0	L		42
49	S onto Mulholland St (*Nauvoo)	1	0	M	CGLQR	40
50	L onto Durphy St/SH 96	11.9	3	M		39
61	R onto US 136 (*Hamilton)	0.7	0	M	CLR	28
62	L at SL onto Warsaw Rd/CR 32/N 6th St	4.8	0	M		27
67	R onto Main St (*Warsaw)	0.6		L	CGQR	22
68	L onto Water St/CR 12/CR 7/E500 St	20	0	L		21
88	L at SS onto N2150/CR 6	1.4	0	L		1
89	*Ursa is 1 mile past the MRT turn onto E603 Rd Ln/Bottom Rd					0

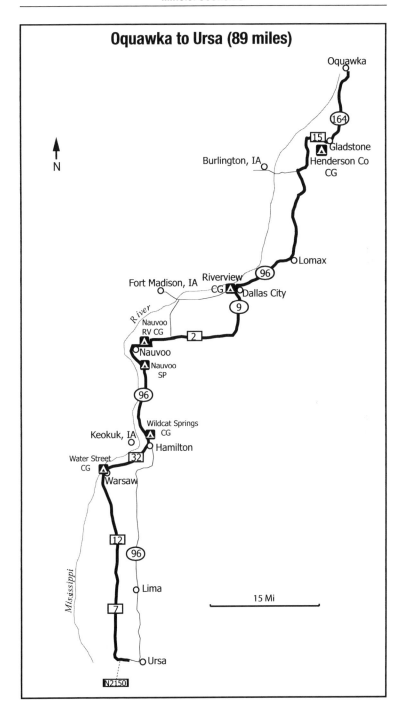

Oquawka to Ursa (89 miles)

Oquawka

164

15

Gladstone

Burlington, IA

Henderson Co
CG

N

Lomax

96

Riverview

Fort Madison, IA

CG Dallas City

9

River

Nauvoo
RV CG

2

Nauvoo

Nauvoo
SP

96

Wildcat Springs

Keokuk, IA   CG

Hamilton

Water Street

32

CG

Warsaw

12

96

Mississippi

Lima

15 Mi

7

Ursa

N2150

Illinois: Section 4
Ursa to Hamburg (79 miles)

Section 4 begins at the E603 turn, off of N2150. This road is later called Bottom Road, then Bonansigna Drive, and as you enter the town of Quincy it is named Bayview Drive. Immediately after Bayview Drive curves into Broadway Street, the MRT takes a quick right onto Front Street. Front Street is bordered by a city park on the riverside and restaurants on the left. There was construction in progress at the time I rode through, so there will probably be more businesses here in the future. It is great that the MRT avoids the busy congestion of the city by routing cyclists through this pleasant riverfront district. From the view on Front Street you can see an example of both a truss bridge, (Quincy Memorial Bridge) and a cable-stayed bridge, (Bayview Bridge). It is unlawful to ride a bicycle across either bridge.

If you would like to see more of Quincy, continue straight on Broadway Street to reach the downtown area. A good start for your tour would be to turn right at 4th Street and ride 2 blocks to Washington Park. This was the city's original central square laid out in 1825 by Quincy's founder, John Wood. The park has a bronze relief sculpture to commemorate this as the site of the sixth debate between Abraham Lincoln and Stephen A. Douglas.

Quincy is also renowned for its architecture. The intersection of Maine Street and 16th Street is one of the ten most architecturally significant corners in the country. The Quincy Museum is also located on this corner. South of Quincy the MRT passes a sign for the Stone Arch Bridge, considered to be one of the most historic bridges in America. If you take this short side trip you will see this 1899 bridge over Curtis Creek. Visit the Tourist Information Center at 532 Gardner Expressway to discover more interesting sights to see in the area.

After following the MRT out of Quincy, when you reach the left turn onto SH 106, you can turn right onto I-72 to cross the MR into Hannibal, Missouri. This is the only section of interstate in Illinois that allows bicycles. Even with the high speeds of interstate traffic, the wide shoulder makes this is a biker-friendly river crossing. Currently Hannibal is the northern most section of the MRT in Missouri.

Once you begin riding SH 106, the best word to describe the route is "flat." So find a comfortable cadence and enjoy your ride across this long, straight stretch of road.

As you ride through the small town of Kinderhook be sure to visit the post office. It was named one of the twelve most unique post offices in the country. In the town of Pleasant Hill, you can turn off of the MRT to the Great River Road Campground, where camping is only $5. To reach the campground, turn right onto Main Street, then ride $1/2$ mile and turn right onto Fairground Road. The MRT continues south of Pleasant Hill on SH 96. After 13 miles, SH 96 turns left, but our route continues straight on CR 2, to the town of Hamburg. This route is also referred to as the Mississippi River Road.

Camping

*Valley View CG
2300 Bonansigna Dr
Quincy, IL
217-222-7229

Great River Road CG
302 Fairground Rd
Pleasant Hill, IL
217-734-2113

Lodging

*Days Inn
200 Maine St
Quincy, IL
217-223-6610

Super 8
224 N 36th St
Quincy, IL
217-228-8808

Cooper Adams House
1122 Kentucky St
Quincy, IL
217-222-8660

*Rail Splitter Inn
115 Hwy 106
Hull, IL
217-432-5417

*BJ Guesthouse
208 E Quincy St. (SH 96)
Pleasant Hill, IL
217-734-2332

Baytown Guesthouse
Hwy 96
Mozier, IL
618-232-1223
(2 night min @ $49)

Bike Shops

Madison & Davis Bicycle
912 S 8th St
Quincy, IL
217-222-7276

Cool Byke LLC
116 N 3rd St
Hannibal, MO
573-248-1560

Ursa to Hamburg (79 miles)

Miles N/S	Directions	Dist	S	T	Services	Miles S/N
0	R onto E603 Rd Ln/CR 7/Bottom Rd	7.7	0	L		79
8	S onto Bonansigna Dr/Bayview Dr	1.9	2	L		71
10	L at SS onto Broadway St then quick R onto Front St (*Quincy)	0.7	0	L	GLQR	69
10	L onto Jefferson St then immediate R onto Gardner Expy/SH 57/E1083 Rd	11.8	1	H		68
22	R onto 1100E/Fall Creek Rd/322nd Ave	5	0	M		57
27	L onto SH 106	8.2	1	M		52
35	S onto SH 96/SH 106 (*Hull)	2.8	0	M	LR	43
38	R onto SH 96 (*Kinderhook)	36.6	0	M	QR	41
	*New Canton				QR	
	*Atlas				QR	
	*Pleasant Hill			0	M CQLR	
	*Mozier				R	
75	S onto Mississippi River Road/CR 2 to Hamburg	3.9	0	L		4
79	*Hamburg				R	0

Bronze statue in Nauvoo, Illinois, of Joseph and Hyrum Smith, with the Mississippi River in the background.

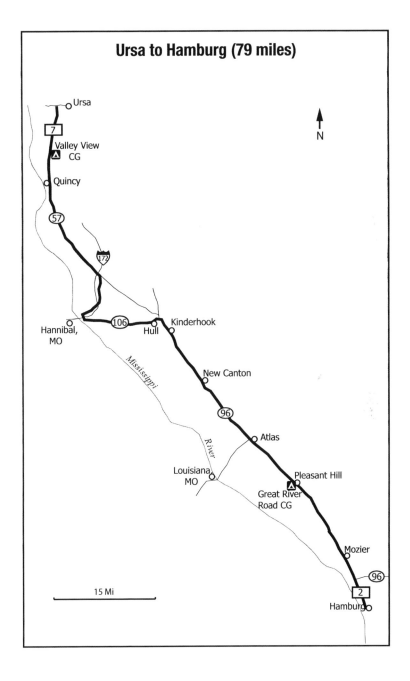

Ursa to Hamburg (79 miles)

Ursa

7

Valley View
CG

Quincy

57

172

106 Kinderhook
Hannibal, Hull
MO

Mississippi

New Canton

96

Atlas

Louisiana
MO   Pleasant Hill
Great River
Road CG

River

Mozier

96

15 Mi   2
Hamburg

N

Illinois: Section 5
Hamburg to Cahokia (79 miles)

There is a lot to see on this section of the MRT. South of Hamburg the trail passes wooded wetlands in the Two Rivers National Wildlife Refuge, offering great opportunities for viewing waterfowl. As you top a rise in the rolling countryside you have views of the MR, and if your vantage point were slightly higher, you could see the Missouri River that is only 6 miles beyond the MR. For the next 30 miles the MRT follows a long peninsula formed by the Illinois and Mississippi rivers, routing you through small towns with fruit markets that sell locally grown produce. The road passes by two ferry landings—for a side trip across the MR into Missouri—before reaching the Brussels Ferry that crosses the Illinois River.

The MRT uses the Brussels Ferry to reach SH 100. A 2-mile ride to the left will take cyclists to the Pere Marquette State Park. The park offers camping, lodging, and a visitor center with displays and exhibits on the rich history of the area. The MRT turns right when you leave the ferry, and after 1 mile it joins the Sam Vadalabene Bike Trail. The bikeway actually begins at the state park, and travels south following a combination of separated bike paths and painted bike lanes for 21 miles to the town of Alton. Much of the bikeway is bordered by 300-foot limestone bluffs on one side and the MR on the other.

There are several interesting attractions along the bikeway; the first one you pass is Marquette Monument. This site has a 7'6" cross, cut from dolomite rock, mounted on a ledge overlooking the Illinois River. The monument commemorates Jacques Marquette as the first European to land in Illinois. The bikeway also routes cyclists through several picturesque river towns that offer food and lodging. Be sure to include a tour of Elsah—often called "the town that time forgot"—and take a break to enjoy a piece of homemade pie at My Just Desserts.

At the southern end of the Sam Vadalabene Bike Trail, you enter the town of Alton. Stop to view the Piasa Bird, a reproduction of a Native American petroglyph painted on the bluff. The Alton Visitor Center is located at the corner of Broadway Street and Landmarks Boulevard. The MRT turns right at this intersection, into a casino parking lot. Veer to your left as you cross the parking lot, to reach the entrance for the Confluence Trail. This is an 18-mile separated paved bike path—with the exception of a short section of gravel near Chain of Rocks Bridge—that follows the top of the MR levee.

Reproduction of Native American Piasa Bird petroglyph, painted on a bluff north of Alton, Illinois.

Shortly after beginning the ride on the Confluence Trail, you pass the National Great Rivers Museum. This museum is more interactive than most museums, utilizing simulators and computers to tell the history of the MR. Another major stop along the bike path is the Lewis and Clark State Historic Site. The site includes a beautiful modern museum with many interesting interactive displays and exhibits that focus on the explorers' adventures in the Illinois area. The Interpretative Center includes a 55-foot full-scale replica of a keel boat, like those used on the expedition. This is definitely another RS.

The MRT continues on the riverside of the center. By following SH 3, cyclists can avoid the gravel section of the MRT and rejoin the route at 20th Street.

If you choose to continue on the MRT, the path routes you on top of the levee bordering the Chain of Rocks Canal. This is a manmade 8-mile-long canal, built in the 1950s and 1960s to bypass the only remaining impediment preventing a reliable navigation channel on the MR between St. Paul, Minnesota, and New Orleans, Louisiana. This impediment, known as the Chain of Rocks Reach, is a series of rock ledges beginning north of St. Louis that makes navigation extremely dangerous during low water levels. The lock on this canal moves more cargo than any other navigation structure on the MR.

When the Confluence Trail passes under the first of two bridges, cyclists can take a side trip to the Chain of Rocks Bridge by following the Chouteau Place Road down the left of the levee bank to Chain of Rocks Road. You then follow the bridge over the canal and on to the Chain of Rocks Bridge. This is a bike/pedestrian-only bridge that crosses the MR and joins the Riverfront Trail on the Missouri side of the river. You can read the "Missouri Section 2" of this guide for more on this area. If you are seeking lodging or camping, you can turn left on Chain of Rocks Road, instead of crossing the canal bridge. A short ride will take you to motels and the camping listed for Granite City in the services section of this guidebook.

The Confluence Trail continues past the two bridges, then leaves the levee to parallel SH 3 for a couple of miles before ending at 20th Street. Once you are on SH 3, be sure to veer left at the intersection with McKinley Bridge. This is a busy area, and it is easy to make a wrong turn onto the bridge. I did.

At this point the MRT routes you through urban neighborhoods in East St. Louis. Occasionally along the ride you get a glimpse of Gateway Arch across the river in St. Louis. There is a wide choice of places to eat along the route. As 9th Street crosses St. Louis Avenue, the Royal Inn is only 1 block to your left. The route also passes the Cahokia RV Parque campground.

Camping

Pere Marquette CG/Lodge	KOA	Cahokia RV Parque
Route 100	3157 Chain of Rocks Rd	4060 Mississippi Ave
Grafton, IL	Granite City, IL	East St. Louis, IL
618-786-2331	618-931-5160	618-332-7700

Lodging

Ruebel Hotel	Green Tree Inn	Super 8 Motel
217 E Main St	15 Mill St	1800 Homer Adams Pkw
Grafton, IL	Elsah, IL	Alton, IL
618-786-2315	618-374-2821	618-465-8885
Hotel Stratford	Canal Motel	Royal Inn
229 Market St	3317 Chain of Rocks Rd	320 N 10th St
Alton, IL	Granite City, IL	East St. Louis, IL
618-465-2700	618-931-0744	618-482-5040

Bike Shops

Eddie's Bicycle Shop
3320 Fernwood Ave
Alton, IL
618-465-6755

Breeze Bikes
3809 Pontoon Rd
Granite City, IL
618-797-0434

Hamburg to Cahokia (79 miles)

Miles N/S	Directions	Dist	S	T	Services	Miles S/N
	*Hamburg					
0	Mississippi River Road(MRR)/CR 2	20.7				79
	*Gilead					59
	*Batchtown					59
	*Winfield Ferry					59
21	L onto Schleeper Rd	2	0	M		59
23	R onto Illinois River Road	1	0	M		57
24	L at SS Prosker Ln/Main St/Illinois River Road (IRR)(*Brussels)	7.5	0	M	QR	56
	*Golden Eagle Ferry to MO					48
	*Brussels Ferry					48
31	R onto SH 100	0.9	0	M	C	48
32	L onto Graham Hollow Rd then R onto Sam Vadalabene Bikeway	17.6	P	L		47
	*Grafton)				QR	30
	*Elsah				LR	30
50	L onto SH 100/Broadway St (*Alton)	2.6	0	M	GLQR	30
52	R at SL onto Landmarks Blvd	0.3	0	M		27
53	L to begin Confluence Trail.	16	P	L		27
	*Lock & Dam 26 museum					11
	*Lewis & Clark Visitor Center					11
	*L onto Chouteau Pl Rd to access Chain of Rocks Bridge. The MRT continues on levee.				C	11
69	L at locked gate on levee path	0.3	0	L		11
69	R onto bike path then cross the road to follow bike path.	2.1	P	L		11
	*Granite City		P	L	GLQR	8
	Confluence Trail ends at W 20th St		0	L		8
71	R onto SH 3	2.8	3	H		8
74	R at SS onto Lincoln Ave/SH3 (*Venice)	0.1	0	H		6
74	R onto 4th St/SH 3	0.5	0	H		6
74	R onto SH 3/2nd St/St Clair Ave	2.7	1	H		5
77	R onto 9th St (*East St. Louis)	1	0	M		2
78	R at SS onto Broadway (1 block)	0	0	M		1
78	L onto 8th St/Mississippi Ave	1.3	0	M		1
79	L at SL onto SH 3					0
	*Cahokia				CLR	

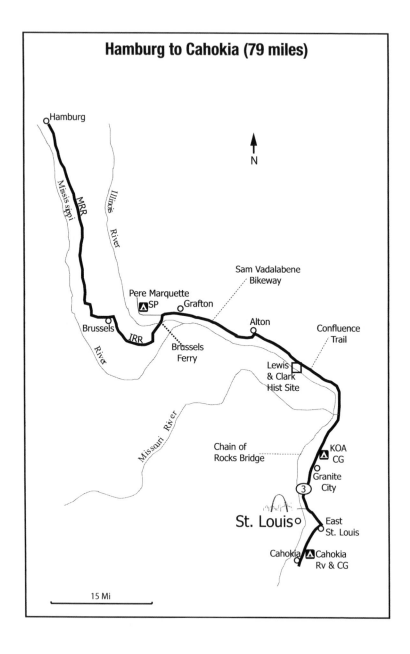

Illinois: Section 6
Cahokia to Neunert (92 miles)

SH 3 is a busy four-lane road as you leave Cahokia, with only a 1-foot shoulder. Use caution in this area. Once the East St. Louis suburban communities are behind you, the MRT routes cyclists back into rural farm land. The flood plain you ride through in this area is referred to as the American Bottoms. This is a strip of river bottoms, ranging from 2 to 9 miles in width, formed within the tall bluffs on both the Missouri and Illinois sides of the MR. Early European settlers were attracted to the area by the rich soil in this bottom land. Later, levees and drainage canals were constructed to control flooding of the MR. However, as the village of Valmeyer can attest to, even man's best efforts do not always control the mighty river. During the Great Flood of 1993 the levees protecting the village were overtopped. For two months a river flowed through the middle of town. As the MRT routes you through Valmeyer, you get a first-hand look at how the community leaders dealt with the MR. They relocated the town to a bluff overlooking the river.

As you ride along Bluff Road, the route passes long stretches of the 80-mile bluff wall of the American Bottoms. You pass many large tunnels in the bluff made by mining operations in the region. The village of Maeystown is located in this area. Although the town is not on the MRT, you can take a 2-mile side trip to visit this interesting community. Maeystown was originally founded by Germans and remained exclusively German for decades. There are several shops, a bed-and-breakfast, and a tavern still remaining that celebrates this German heritage.

As you ride through the village of Prairie du Rocher, a 4-mile side trip will take you to Fort de Chartres. This is a partially reconstructed stone fort built by the French between 1720 and 1763 that provides a glimpse of life in Illinois under the French regime. There are events scheduled at the fort that encourage visitor participation—for both kids and adults—and make learning about the history of the area a fun experience. The largest and most popular event at the fort is the annual Rendezvous, a re-creation of the traditional French fur-trapper's holiday of the eighteenth century. The fort is open at no charge, 9 a.m. to 5 p.m., Wednesday through Sunday.

South of Prairie du Rocher, in the town of Modoc, you have an option of riding 4 miles on Modoc Ferry Road to reach a ferry that crosses the MR to historic Ste. Genevieve, Missouri. The ferry operates daily from 6 a.m. to 6 p.m., and charges $3 per-bicycle.

As you continue along the MRT, the route passes the restored home of Pierre Menard, a French Canadian who served as the Illinois Territory's first lieutenant governor. This fine example of French Creole-style architecture is open daily for tours.

If you are planning to camp at Kaskaskia State Park, turn left on the road that borders the Pierre Menard home, and shortly after this, turn left again onto Park Road. The park is located high on a bluff, overlooking the MR. There are interpretative displays marking the location of the fort that once stood here, but all that remains now are the earthen embankments of its foundation. The main attraction of the area is the magnificent view of the river below. In Section 3 of the Missouri chapter of this guide, I explained how the residents of Kaskaskia Village were forced to abandon the town when the MR altered its course. The cemetery in the park contains gravesites that were relocated from the town. From the vantage point in the park, both the old and new channels of the MR are visible. With the view, the history, and the campground, this is a RS, even with the steep climb up Park Road.

As you pass the Menard Correctional Center, look across the MR, where you can see the original channel of the river before its altered course overtook the Kaskaskia River channel. In Chester, as in many of the communities the MRT passes, the route skirts the town to avoid traffic. To access the business district, turn left onto Branch Street and follow it to SH 150, where several eating establishments are located. The Stone House lodging, listed under services, is located within two-tenths of a mile from the MRT. It can easily be reached by turning left off of Kaskaskia Street onto Ferry Street, then right onto Randolph Street. This is a beautiful structure that was originally a First Presbyterian Church, until lightning destroyed the bell tower in 1921.

South of Chester the MRT routes cyclists through farmland and patches of interspersed wetlands. This area is still part of the Mississippi Byway, used by migrating birds. The wooded wetlands and the crops raised in these fields make this a popular stop for waterfowl, and great viewing opportunities for you.

Camping

Cahokia RV Parque
4060 Mississippi Ave
Cahokia, IL
618-332-7700

Fort Kaskaskia State CG
4372 Park Road
Ellis Grove, IL
618-859-3741

Randolph Co Conservation CG
4301 S Lake Dr
Chester, IL
618-826-2706

Lodging

Trails End Motel
600 Water St
Cahokia, IL
618-337-2010

Corner George Inn
1101 Main St
Maeystown, IL
618-458-6660
(off the MRT route)

La Maison du Rocher Inn
215 Duclos St
Prairie du Rocher, IL
618-284-3463

The Stone House
509 Harrison St
Chester, IL
618-604-9106

Best Western Inn
2150 State St
Chester, IL
618-826-3034

Hi-3 Motel
827 Lehman Dr
Chester, IL
618-826-4415

Bike Shops

Columbia Bike Shop
109 N Rapp Ave
Columbia, IL
618-281-6910

View of the Mississippi River from high upon the bluff at Kaskaskia State Park.

Cahokia to Neunert (92 miles)

Miles N/S	Directions	Dist	S	T	Services	Miles S/N
	*Cahokia				CLR	
0	L at SL onto SH 3	4.7	1	H		92
5	R onto Stolle Rd/Main St (*Dupo)	2.2	0	M	QR	87
7	Veer L staying on S Main St	0.8	0	M		85
8	S onto Old Route 3 (cross over I-55)	3.2	0	M		84
11	R at SS onto Palmer Rd (*Columbia)	0.4	0	M	GR	81
11	Veer L onto Bluff Rd/CR 6	6.9	0	M		80
18	Veer R onto Levee Rd (no sign)	1	0	M		73
19	Veer L onto Bluff Rd	4	0	M		72
23	R onto Old Bluff Rd/Lake St	2.3	0	M		68
26	L onto Main St (*Valmeyer)	0.4	0	M		66
26	R onto Bluff Rd/CR 3	6.6	0	L		66
	*Side trip to Maeystown Rd 2 miles					
33	R onto Bluff Rd	12.8	0	L		59
45	R at SS onto Henry St/SH 155 (*Prairie du Rocher)	0.1	0	M	QR	46
45	L onto Market St/Bluff Rd/CR 7 (*Modoc)	4.3	0	M		46
50	L onto Bluff Rd/Roots Rd	7.9	0	L		42
58	R onto SH 3	0.3	0	L		34
58	R onto Branch St	0.1	0	L		34
58	L onto Main St (*Ellis Grove)	0.3	0	L	QR	34
58	R onto 1st St/Riley Lake Rd/Kaskaskia Rd	9.8	0	M		33
	*L to Fort Kaskaskia Historic Park		0		C	
	*Chester				CGLQR	
68	Veer R onto SH 3/Truck Bypass	3.1	0	M		24
71	R at SS onto SH 3	7.8	1	H		20
79	R onto Levee Rd	0.2	0	L		13
79	L onto Cora Rd (*Cora)	1.1	0	L		12
80	L onto Levee Rd	1.4	0	L		11
82	L onto Little Levee Rd	2.1	0	L		10
84	L onto Levee Rd	2	0	L		8
86	L onto Indian Ridge Rd/CR 9	2.7	0	L		6
89	R at SS onto Neunert Rd/CR 9	3.1	0	L		3
92	*Neunert				R	0

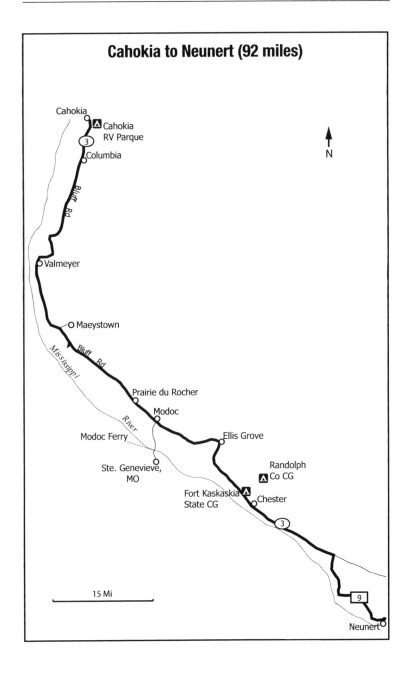

Cahokia to Neunert (92 miles)

Cahokia
Cahokia RV Parque
③
Columbia
Bluff Rd
Valmeyer
Maeystown
Bluff Rd
Mississippi
Prairie du Rocher
Modoc
River
Modoc Ferry
Ellis Grove
Ste. Genevieve, MO
Randolph Co CG
Fort Kaskaskia State CG
Chester
③
9
Neunert

15 Mi

N

Illinois: Section 7
Neunert to Cairo (74 miles)

Before you leave Neunert, you might consider having a good meal at the Bottoms Up Bar & Grill. There are no services after Neunert until you reach Jonesboro, 34 miles away. I was told the grill has the best fried chicken in the state. Unfortunately, it was closed when I rode through.

As it continues south, the MRT routes cyclists through a haunted town. Grand Tower has been linked to spirits even before Louis Jolliet and Jacques Marquette explored the MR. Native Americans believed that the rapids in the MR at the base of the rocky bluff, now known as Devil's Bake Oven, were the work of evil spirits determined to claim the lives of unwitting victims. The legend of sprits continued in later years, when the town constructed its first iron works factory on top of Devil's Bake Oven. The daughter of the factory's superintendent had a young suitor, of whom the father did not approve. The father bribed the young man into leaving the area, never to return. The daughter, distraught over losing the love of her life, fell ill and soon died. Following her death, visitors to the superintendent's house, which was also located on top of Devil's Bake Oven, reported seeing a strange, mist-like shape walking the halls of the house. These sightings continued long after the house had been razed. It is said that when thunderstorms sweep through the area, the wails and moans of the heart-broken girl sound like blood-curdling screams.

At the town of Wolf Lake, the MRT routes you off of busy SH 3 onto less traveled roads. Leaving the MR corridor behind, you enter woody, hilly terrain as you ride through Trail of Tears State Forest. This is a nice ride through dense forest that extends to the road shoulders. In all there are nine campgrounds within the park boundaries; however, there is only one that is accessible by paved road. You pass this campground 1-mile past the visitor information building.

While in the town of Jonesboro, you can visit Lincoln Memorial Park, site of the third debate between Abraham Lincoln and Stephen A. Douglas for the Illinois senate seat. You might consider parking your bike at the Jonesboro Square and "Walk Where Lincoln Walked," to travel the $^{1}/_{4}$– mile distance to the debate site. Douglas chose to reach the site by buggy.

If you don't mind riding 6 miles off the route, when the MRT reaches the left turn off of SH 127 onto Olive Branch Road, you can turn right onto SH 3 to reach Horseshoe Lake Campground. This is one of my favorite campgrounds in the state. The campground itself is not what sets it apart, although it is nice and does have showers. The lake is what makes it special. The area around the campground is more of a swamp than a lake, with bald cypress, tupelo gums, and swamp cottonwood trees growing in the shallow waters. To reach the campground, turn right onto SH 3 and continue for eight-tenths of a mile, next turn left onto Promised Land Road and ride another 3 miles, then turn right on an unnamed road for 2 miles. This last 2 miles of the ride borders the lake with fantastic views of the lake.

As you enter the town of Mound City, the MRT passes a National Cemetery that was constructed in 1864. There are interesting historical monuments and memorials to visit in the cemetery. The memorial I enjoyed most was the "Bivouac of the Dead," consisting of seven plaques that border the avenue through the cemetery. Each plaque is inscribed with a verse from that famous poem by Theodore O'Hara. This elegant literary memorialization of fallen soldiers was so effective in expressing the feelings of sorrow over the loss of life in war that Quartermaster General Montgomery C. Meigs directed that lines from the poem grace the entrance to Arlington National Cemetery.

Cairo marks the end of the MRT in the state of Illinois. This once-thriving town is now little more than a ghost town. The buildings still remain from its glory days, when it was a major river town at the confluence of the Ohio and Mississippi rivers, but they are now empty. However, this makes for an interesting bike tour of the city to view the remnants of Cairo's past grandeur.

As you follow the MRT out of Cairo, it crosses the Ohio River into the state of Kentucky on the SH 51 bridge. This is a busy narrow bridge with heavy truck traffic. It is recommended that cyclists request a police escort for the crossing. If this is not possible, you might try asking someone with a pickup to haul you across the bridge. If these are impractical options, use extreme caution during the crossing.

Camping

*Devil's Backbone Park CG
Brunkhorst Ave
Grand Tower, IL
618-684-6192

Pine Hills CG
Off of State Forest Rd
Wolf Lake, IL
618-833-8576
(1 mile on gravel rd)

*Trail of Tears State CG
3240 State Forest Rd
Wolf Lake, IL
618-833-4910
(1 mile past info center)

Horseshoe Lake CG
Box 85
Miller City, IL
618-776-5689
(off MRT route)

*Garden Inn & RV Park
US 51 & SH 3
Cairo, IL
618-734-9554

*Fort Defiance SP
US 60 & SH 51
Cairo, IL
618-734-4127
(just past bridge)

Lodging

*Iron Mountain B&B
2360 Hwy 127 N
Jonesboro, IL
618-833-5613

*Forest View Lodge
1500 State Rt 127 N
Jonesboro, IL
618-833-1500

Lincoln Motel
601 E Broad St
Jonesboro, IL
618-833-2181

Hummingbird Hollow B&B
31317 McDaniel School Rd
Tamms, IL
618-747-2316

*Belvedere Motel
3901 Sycamore St
Cairo, IL
618-734-4020

Days Inn
13201 Kessler Rd
Cairo, IL
618-734-0215

Bike Shops

The Bike Surgeon
404 S Illinois Ave
Carbondale, IL
618-457-4521

Carbondale Cycle Shop
303 S Illinois Ave
Carbondale, IL
618-549-6863

Phoenix Cycles
300 S Illinois Ave
Carbondale, IL
618-549-3612

Neunert to Cairo (74 miles)

Miles N/S	Directions	Dist	S	T	Services	Miles S/N
	*Neunert					
0	R at SS onto Neunert Rd/CR 9	3.7	0	L		74
4	R onto Main St/Gorham Rd (*Gorham)	1.6	2	L		70
5	R onto SH 3	3.4	0	M		68
9	R onto Power Plant Rd	1.8	0	L		65
11	L onto street after 3rd St Ext	0.7	0	L		63
11	R onto 25th St	0.1	0	L		62
11	L onto 5th Ave	0.3	0	L		62
12	R at SS onto 20th St	0	0	L		62
12	L onto Brunkhorst St	1	0	L		62
13	L onto Front St (*Grand Tower)	0.5	0	L	CQR	61
13	R onto Island Rd	0.5	0	L		60
14	L onto Upper Chute Rd	1	0	L		60
15	R at SS onto SH 3	8.6	0	H		59
23	L onto State Forest Rd/CR 13 (*Wolf Lake)	7.5	0	L		50
	*Trail of Tears State Forest info center				C	
31	R onto SH 127	1.2	0	M		43
32	L onto SH 127/SH 146	2.6	2	M		42
35	R onto SH 127 (*Jonesboro)	15.4	1	M	GLQR	39
50	R onto Front St (*Tamms)	1.6	1	M	QR	24
52	R at SS onto SH 127	6.3	1	M		22
58	L onto Olive Branch Rd/CR 6/Sycamore St	4.7	0	M		16
63	R onto Blanche St/US 51/SH 37 (*Mounds)	2.6	0	M	Q	11
65	R onto US 51/SH 37	3.5	1	H		8
69	L onto US 51/Sycamore St/Washington Ave (*Cairo)	4.2	0	H	CGLQR	5
73	L onto SH 51 to cross Mississippi River into Kentucky	0.7				1
74	Enter Kentucky					0

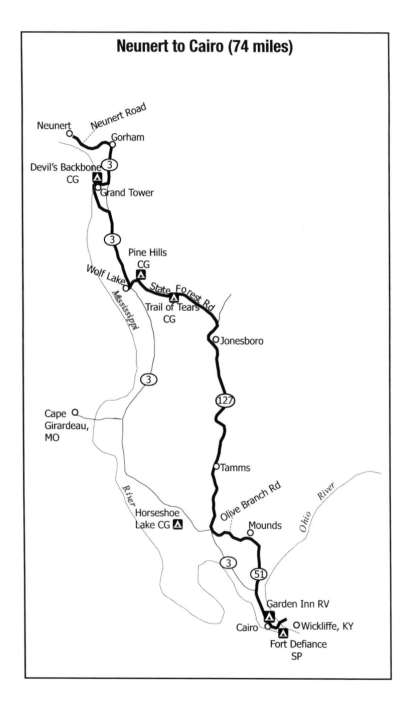

Neunert to Cairo (74 miles)

Neunert
Neunert Road
Gorham
Devil's Backbone CG
③
Grand Tower
③
Pine Hills CG
Wolf Lake
State Forest Rd
Trail of Tears CG
Mississippi
Jonesboro
③
127
Cape Girardeau, MO
Tamms
River
Olive Branch Rd
Ohio River
Horseshoe Lake CG
Mounds
③
51
Garden Inn RV
Cairo
Wickliffe, KY
Fort Defiance SP

MISSOURI

The MRT in Missouri does not begin at its northern border, with the state of Iowa. Instead, the route begins in Hannibal, Missouri, crossing over from the state of Illinois. Also, rather than extending to its southern border with Arkansas, the MRT crosses back over the MR into the state of Kentucky on the Dorena-Hickman Ferry. There are plans for future expansion of the trail to Missouri's northern and southern borders; however, the current route still offers an enjoyable 348-mile ride through the state.

The northern half of the MRT routes cyclists through hilly countryside, with climbs reaching 400 feet in elevation gains. This rollercoaster ride gradually begins to level out in the central section of the state, and continues this trend as the route reaches the Mississippi River delta of the state's "Bootheel" region.

There is a great deal of interesting history in the quaint river towns the MRT passes through. The influence of the state's early French settlers can be found not just in the towns and architecture, but also in the names of the creeks and other waterways you cross.

There are several biker-friendly bridges and ferries that cross the MR for planning a multiple-day loop tour or to just get a different perspective of the river from the Illinois MRT. There are MRT signs installed on the southern section of the trail, from St. Louis to Dorena.

Missouri: Section 1
Hannibal to St. Charles (105 miles)

The MRT enters the state of Missouri from the state of Illinois by way of the biker-friendly US 36 Bridge. After crossing the MR, follow the first exit for SH 79 south. This will take you into Hannibal, a colorful town perched on the banks of the MR. This is the boyhood home of Samuel Clemens, better known as Mark Twain, one of America's best-loved authors. The city has preserved several of the buildings from young Clemens' neighborhood. On a walking tour, you can relive many of the adventures of Tom Sawyer and Huckleberry Finn as you identify Clemens' inspiration for his stories, such as the white picket fence Tom tricked his friends into painting. There are eight buildings on the tour, including Clemens' boyhood home, the Becky Thatcher Home, and the Huckleberry Finn House.

The town also has other attractions for visitors that are not associated with Samuel Clemens. You can find information on these at the Visitor Center, located at 505 North Third Street, next to the Hotel Clemens. The town of Hannibal is a RS. It is made even more enjoyable with a stop at the Java Jive for a refreshing Italian soda.

Just south of Hannibal, there is a turn off of SH 79 for a steep climb to Lovers' Leap. In 1844, William Miller prophesied the Second Coming of Christ. He and other Millerites in the area abandoned their crops and stores, put on long, white robes, and gathered at Lovers' Leap to await Christ's return. The beautiful bluff setting would have been, or yet may still be, a great location for His return.

During the initial 40 miles of the Missouri MRT, cyclists will be riding over rolling hills with 200–300 foot elevation gains. From the tops of these climbs you will see patches of wooded plots and an occasional glimpse of the MR, but most of your views will be of the large farm fields that dominate the area. There is a paved bike lane from Louisiana to Clarksville; however, with the exception of a few additional short stretches, most of the shoulders on this section of the MRT are not paved. Since much of this section has a wide gravel shoulder in place, hopefully someday its shoulders will be paved.

Five miles north of the town of Ashburn, the MRT passes the Edward Anderson Wildlife Area. If you are in need of a convenient place to pitch your tent, camping is allowed in the parking lot for the wildlife area. There is no water or toilet—in truth, it isn't much more than a graded flat spot—but the price fits even my budget. Free. The Ted Shanks Conservation Area also offers camping, but the campgrounds are 5 miles off of SH 79 on CR TT, with 2 miles of this on gravel.

The MRT routes cyclists through a region with noticeable touches of Southern charm and style that have earned it the nickname of "Little Dixie." Louisiana, Missouri, is part of the "Little Dixie" region. It is a pleasant town to park your bike and take an enjoyable walking tour. The outer walls of many of the historical buildings in town have painted murals that depict the area's historical past. Your tour of the town should also include Henderson Riverfront Park, which has bluff views of the MR and the US 54 Bridge (which does not include a shoulder for cyclists), to Illinois. Henderson Riverfront Park has water and restrooms, and does allow tent camping for cyclists.

Farther south on SH 79 in the town of Clarksville, you'll reach the geographical halfway-point between the Canadian border and the Gulf of Mexico. Clarksville provides a close vantage point for viewing the MR, with 1st Street located along the banks of the river. The town has several shops displaying arts and crafts by local artists.

Clarksville has a long association with bicycling. George Knightly, a blacksmith, started Missouri's first bicycle factory in this town, and in 1867 the first national bike race was held on nearby Old Belt Road. It is no surprise that this bicycle-oriented area would have the first paved bike lane on SH 79.

After leaving Clarksville, the traffic begins to intensify as you ride closer to the suburbs of St. Louis. Use extreme caution on this stretch. As I mentioned earlier, most of the highway shoulders are gravel. When you reach the south end of Salt River Road, at the turn for CR C, a 1-mile detour to the right will take you to full services in the St. Peters community.

After turning off of Salt River Road, the MRT routes you away from the busy suburbs into rural farmland once again. CR B routes you by a turn for the Golden Eagle Ferry. This ferry crosses the MR into the state of Illinois. It operates daily from 8 a.m. to 9 p.m. If you take this ferry, then ride 10 miles in Illinois, you can take the Brussels Ferry across the Illinois River. You really need both a Missouri and an Illinois state map to understand that within a 20-mile ride, you could cross three major rivers: the Missouri, the Mississippi, and the Illinois. I had already ridden the MRT in Missouri when I rode through Illinois. As I was approaching the Brussels Ferry in Illinois, I passed the sign for the Golden Eagle Ferry. I thought I remembered something about this ferry from my Missouri ride. As soon as I reached camp in Pere Marquette State Park that evening, I pulled out my Missouri and Illinois maps. I had no idea that these tributaries emptied into the MR within 20 miles of each other. I found this very interesting, but then after having ridden the MRT, I am fascinated by many facets of this great river.

When you reach the turn for the MRT onto Hawning Road, if you continue straight on SH 94 for another 3 miles you will reach the Katy Trail State Park. At 225 miles, the Katy Trail is America's longest "rails-to-trails" project. There is no camping at the park, or any place else in this area, but since the park is located in Historic St. Charles there is a wide selection of lodging establishments to choose from. If you are looking for economical lodging conveniently located to the MRT, the Sundermeier RV Park rents cabins at a reasonable rate. To reach the RV park, continue past the Hawning Road turn for about another mile, then turn left onto Transit Street. This RV park also puts you within a short walk to the shops and restaurants of the historical district, which is a RS.

Boyhood home of Mark Twain, located in Hannibal, Missouri.

Camping

*Mark Twain Cave CG
300 Cave Hollow Road
Hannibal, MO
573-221-1656

Henderson Riverfront Pk
Georgia Street
Louisiana, MO

*Silo Public Access CG
Hwy 79, 4 miles north of
Clarksville, MO
Free Primitive camping

Lodging

*Hotel Clemens
401 N. 3rd St
Hannibal, MO
573-248-1150

Robard's Mansion B&B
215 N. 6th St
Hannibal, MO
573-248-1218

*River's Edge Motel
201 Mansion St
Louisiana, MO
573-754-4522

Eagle's Nest Inn
221 Georgia St
Louisiana, MO
573-754-9888

Cedarcrest Manor B&B
813 South 4th Street
Clarksville, MO
573-242-3310

*Hillcrest Motel
3407 N Hwy 79
Elsberry, MO
573-898-2121

Drury Inn
170 Westfield Dr
St. Peters, MO
636-397-9700

Sundermeier Cabins
111 Transit St
St. Charles, MO
800-929-0832

Lococohouse II B&B
1309 N Fifth St
St. Charles, MO
636-946-0619

Comfort Suites
1400 S. Fifth St
St. Charles, MO
636-949-0694

Best Western Motel
1377 S 5th St
St. Charles, MO
636-916-3000

Victorian Memories B&B
709 N 4th St
St. Charles, MO
636-940-8111

Bike Shops

Cool Byke LLC
116 N 3rd Street
Hannibal, MO
573-248-1560

Momentum Cycles
384 Mid Rivers Mall Drive
St. Peters, MO
636-397-7433

Momentum Cycles
104 S. Main Street
St. Charles, MO
636-946-7433

Hannibal to St. Charles (105 miles)

Miles N/S	Directions	Dist	S	T	Services	Miles S/N
0	Enter Missouri on US 36, Mark Twain Mem Bridge	0.6	4	H		105
1	L onto SH 79 (take south exit) (*Hannibal)	19.5	0	M		104
20	*Ashburn	14	0	M		85
34	*Louisiana	10.2	5	M	GLQR	71
44	*Clarksville	15.1	5	M	QR	61
59	*Elsberry	12.6	0	H	GLQR	45
72	*Winfield	14.6	0	H	QR	33
87	L onto Salt River Rd.	1.5	8	H		18
88	L onto CR C	4.4	0	L		17
93	R onto CR B	9.2	0	L		12
102	R onto SH 94	0.9	5	M		3
103	L onto Hawning Rd/N River Rd/Lower Bottom Rd	2.2	0	L		2
105	*St. Charles				GLQR	0

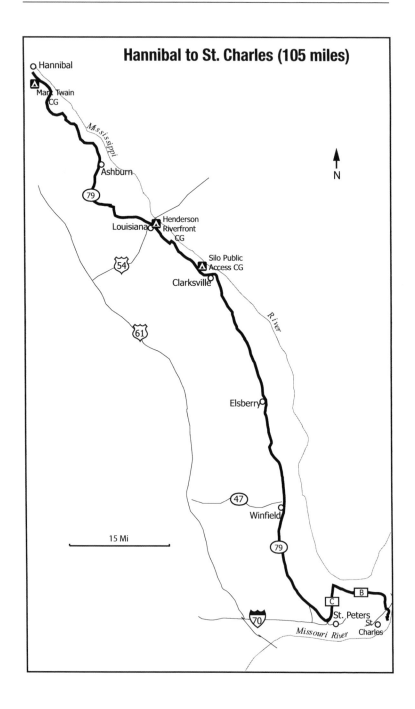

Hannibal to St. Charles (105 miles)

Hannibal

Mark Twain CG

Mississippi

Ashburn

79

Louisiana — Henderson Riverfront CG

54

Silo Public Access CG

Clarksville

61

River

Elsberry

47

Winfield

15 Mi

79

N

B

C

St. Peters

St. Charles

70

Missouri River

Missouri: Section 2
St. Charles to Arnold (49 miles)

This section of the MRT begins in St. Charles on the north side of the Missouri River. The route takes you past Ed Bales Memorial Park, which has restrooms and water, on North River Road. After passing under the SH 370 bridge, the MRT immediately turns right onto a bike path. This paved path will take you to the east bound lanes of the SH 370 bridge. After crossing the Missouri River on this biker-friendly bridge, the MRT turns right onto another bike path. This path circles under the bridge to an unnamed road that will take you to Missouri Bottom Road. For those cyclists traveling south to north, you have your own bike path along the westbound lanes of the SH 370 bridge.

Because this section of the MRT passes through the city of St. Louis and its suburbs, I have increased the scale of the map to add greater detail. The route is straightforward with a limited number of turns, and MRT signs have been installed in this area. However, continue following the Mileage Log to avoid unwanted detours.

After entering the North Riverfront Park off of Riverview Drive, there is a bike path to the left. This is an optional side trip that is not part of the MRT route. By following this path $1^1/_2$ miles upriver, you will reach the Chain of Rocks Bridge. This bridge was the MR crossing for Route 66, the famous highway referred to as "The Mother Road" for the great migration west during the financially turbulent 1930s. There are signs and other interpretative displays on the bridge commemorating this historic period in America's past. The bridge is now closed to motorized traffic, and at 1-mile-long is the world's longest pedestrian and bicycle bridge.

A unique feature of the Chain of Rocks Bridge is the 22-degree turn in the middle. This bend was designed to address concerns that the bridge pylons would present for navigation due to the geology of the area. Part of this concern was related to the extremely hard rock ledge crossing the MR south of the bridge. This is what gives the area the name Chain of Rocks. The Illinois chapter of this guide provides more detail on the Chain of Rocks, for that state was more affected by the rock formation. As you ride across the bridge, notice the two gothic castle-like structures downriver. These are water intakes for the area. The bridge is also a good location to pause and enjoy the excellent view of Gateway Arch and the St. Louis skyline. A visit to the Chain of Rocks is a RS. The bridge also provides a safe bicycle crossing to Granite City, Illinois, for planning a loop tour.

After returning to North Riverfront Park, cyclists exit on one of the jewels of the MRT, the Riverfront Trail. This paved 9-mile bike/pedestrian path travels downriver along the top of the levee and between the levee and the river, providing cyclists with excellent views of the river and the approaching city of St. Louis. As you near the city, the trail passes through enormous flood gates used to seal off the city when the great river's waters become threatening.

The southern end of the Riverfront Trail is located in downtown St. Louis. Shortly after exiting the trail onto Leonor K. Sullivan Boulevard, you reach the base of the 630-foot-tall Gateway Arch, built in 1965 as a monument to westward expansion in the USA. After Captain Henry Miller Shreve sailed down the Ohio River to the MR in 1807, and made the decision to head upriver with his cargo to St. Louis rather than downstream as was the norm at that time, the city became one of the most active ports on the river. Many people and supplies passed through the city during both the gold rush and land rush of the early 1800s, and by 1849 St. Louis became known as the "Gateway to the West."

The city's early growth centered around the steamboat traffic on the MR. If not for the foresight of community leaders, the city would not have survived after the end of the steamboat era. These St. Louis businessmen recognized the threat to their city's future from the major railroad construction taking place in the city of Chicago, Illinois. They sent out a call to engineers, seeking designs for a bridge across the MR. One of the men to respond was James Buchanan Eads. Although Eads had never built a bridge before, his design was accepted. The fact that the Eads Bridge is the oldest remaining bridge across the MR is testimony to the success of his design. Eads played a major role in the development of the MR, not just in the St. Louis area but in correcting the problem of silt buildup as the MR empties into the Gulf of Mexico.

For those who would like to learn more about the area, I suggest stopping at the visitor center, located at 7th and Washington Avenue, 314-342-5160. Also, if you ride a couple of blocks off of Leonor K. Sullivan Boulevard onto Morgan Street, you will find a selection of restaurants. The hotels I have listed are also near this area.

The MRT route south of St. Louis is basically SH 231. However, you will find it easier to follow the street names I have listed in the Mileage Log rather than watching for SH 231 signs. This stretch is marked with MRT signs, and there are some segments with paved shoulders and painted bike lanes. Like the outskirts of most major cities, the communities south of St. Louis blend together, making one continuous string of heavy traffic. On the plus side, there are plenty of dining opportunities for cyclists. The motel I have listed for Arnold is on US 61, less than 1 mile into the next section's Mileage Log.

Camping

N/A

Lodging

Econo Lodge-Riverfront
1100 N 3rd Street
St Louis, MO
314-421-6556

Drury Inn
2 South 4th St
St. Louis, MO
314-231-3003

Hampton Inn
333 Washington Ave
St. Louis, MO
314-621-7900

Hilton Inn
400 Olive St
St. Louis, MO
314-436-0002

*Geandaugh B&B
3835 S Broadway
St. Louis, MO
314-771-5447

*Pleasant View Motel
43101 Jeffco Blvd
Arnold, MO
636-464-3301

Bike Shops

South Side Cyclery
6969 Gravcis
St. Louis, MO
314-481-1120

Alpine Shop
440 N Kirkwood
St. Louis, MO
314-962-7715

A&M Cycle & Supply Co
4282 Arsenal St
St Louis, MO
314-776-1144

Mesa Cycles
1035 S Big Bend Rd
St. Louis, MO
314-645-4447

Maplewood Bicycle
7534 Manchester Rd
St. Louis, MO
314-781-9566

Big Shark Bicycle Co
6133 Delmar Blvd
St. Louis, Mo
314-862-1188

St. Charles to Arnold (49 miles)

Miles N/S	Directions	Dist	S	T	Services	Miles S/N
	*St. Charles					49
0	R onto bike path after riding under SH 370 bridge then circle up and cross Missouri River Bridge SH 370 west bound shoulder.	0.6	8	H		49
1	R onto bike path immediately after crossing Missouri River to circle under bridge then follow unnamed road paralleling ramp for SH 370 East	0.8	P	L		49
1	L onto Missouri Bottom Rd	1	0	M		48
2	R onto Missouri Bottom Rd at junction with Aubuchon Rd	1	0	M		47
3	R onto St Louis Mills Blvd	0.4	0	M		46
4	L onto Taussig Rd	0.2	0	M		46
4	R onto Missouri Bottom Rd	0.3	0	M		45
4	S onto Leafcrest Dr	0.3	0	M		45
5	S onto Missouri Bottom Rd	1.6	0	M		45
6	L onto Fee Fee Rd	0.8	0	M		43
7	R onto James S McDonnell Blvd	2.5	0	M		42
10	L onto Airport Rd	2.2	0	M		40
12	S onto Hereford Ave	0.4	0	M		38
12	S onto Chambers Rd	4.6	0	M		37
17	R onto Chambers Rd SE	0.5	0	M		33
17	L onto Riverview Dr	0.2	0	M		32
17	R onto Riverfront Trail	9	P	L		32
26	L onto Leonor K Sullivan Blvd (*St. Louis)	1.4	3	H	GLQR	23
28	R onto Chouteau Ave	0.4	0	H		22
28	L onto Broadway	0.3	0	H		21
29	R onto 7th Blvd	1	3	H		21
30	R onto Broadway/SH 231	6.7	0	H		20
36	R onto Kingston Rd/SH 231	1.1	3	H		13
37	L onto Telegraph Rd/SH 231	12	3	H		12
49	*Arnold				GLQR	0

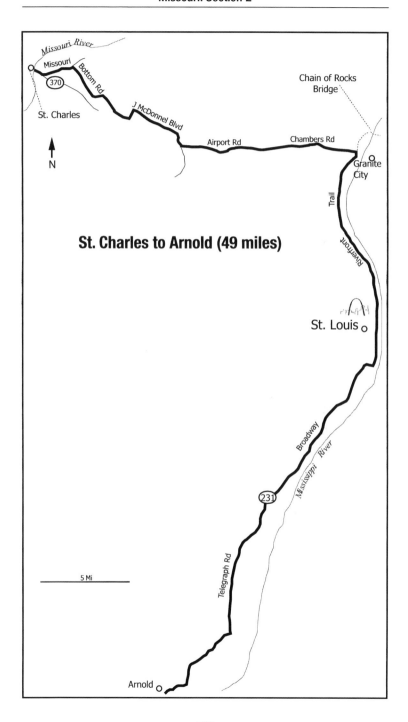

St. Charles to Arnold (49 miles)

Missouri: Section 3
Arnold to Fruitland (90 miles)

The majority of the first 14 miles of this section of the MRT are bordered by commercial businesses, resulting in heavy traffic. There is a shoulder through much of it, but this is not one of the more enjoyable stretches of the MRT. Keep one eye on your mirror for the traffic behind you and the other on the business exits for the traffic merging onto the highway.

There is an interesting attraction in this area that is a RS. As you ride through the community of Imperial, you are within 2 miles of one of the most important archaeological sites in Missouri— the Mastodon State Historical Site. At this site archaeologists first discovered stone weapons along with the bones of American mastodons. This was the first solid evidence of the coexistence of humans and mastodons in eastern North America. The site includes a museum that tells the natural and cultural history of the area, plus a replica of a male adult American mastodon that stands 10 feet tall and 20 feet long. The area also has trails that offer visitors a chance to explore the land where mastodons and Native American hunters once lived. To reach the historical site, turn right off of US 61/67 onto Imperial Main Street. After riding ½ mile, turn right onto West Outer Road. Follow this road another mile to Museum Road, which will take you to the museum.

The stretch of US 61 to Ste. Genevieve goes through rolling hills and farmland. Other than a convenience store north of Bloomsdale, there are no services on this road. With I-55 nearby, traffic is rated low on this road.

There is no convenient camping in this area. The nearest camping is located at the Magnolia Hollow Conservation Area, over 7 miles off of the MRT route. To reach this campground, continue 1½ miles south of Bloomsdale on US 61, then turn left onto CR V. Follow this road for 1 mile, then turn left onto White Sandy Road. After following this road for 6 miles, with the last ½ mile on gravel, you will reach the camping area. This is primitive camping with no fee.

When you are planning the itinerary for your bike tour, be sure to schedule time for exploring Ste. Genevieve, the oldest European settlement west of the MR. Many of the city's earliest residents were French-Canadian, and their influence is present in many of the buildings that have been preserved. The area represents the best example of French colonial architecture in this hemisphere. Nowhere is this influence more evident than in the Bolduc House. Built in 1785, the walls of this structure follow the vertical-log pattern used by the French. The Bolduc House is regarded as one of the most authentically restored Creole houses in the nation. The house and its gardens are open to the public for tours.

The Great River Road Interpretative Center, located in Ste. Genevieve at the corner of Market Street and Main Street, has interpretative displays and literature on the area's history. It also offers a walking tour map of the historic section of the town.

For those cyclists seeking a route for a loop tour, the Ste. Genevieve-Modoc Ferry is a pleasant means for crossing the MR into Illinois. Following an enjoyable boat ride across the river, cyclists then have the option of riding the Illinois MRT either north to the Chain of Rocks Bridge in Granite City or south to the Bill Emerson Memorial Bridge in East Cape Girardeau.

Eight miles south of Ste. Genevieve, in the town of St. Mary, the MRT passes a sign for the Kaskaskia Bell Historic Site. The 650-pound bell was a gift in 1743 to the Mission of the Immaculate Conception Catholic Church and the citizens of the village of Kaskaskia from King Louis XV of France. At that time, the village, often called "The Paris of the West," was the center of French colonial administration for the Middle Mississippi River. Kaskaskia later became Illinois' first state capital.

If you take this 5-mile side trip to Kaskaskia Island, as the area is now known, you will find an example of the devastation the MR can wreak on an area. In the flood of 1881 the MR altered its channel from the west side of Kaskaskia Village to its east side. Following this, the river's waters gradually ate away at the land on which the town was built until eventually its citizens were forced to abandon the town. Now all that remains of this once thriving community, other than a few houses, is a small brick building housing the historic bell and the rebuilt Mission of the Immaculate Conception Catholic Church.

Another attraction on this section of the MRT is the National Shrine of Our Lady of the Miraculous Medal, in the town of Perryville. The shrine is located in Saint Mary's of the Barrens Church. This is a beautiful shrine with Biblical scenes from the scriptures painted on the shrine's dome and the walls of the church.

Camping

Magnolia Hollow CG
White Sandy Rd
Bloomsdale, MO
See directions in text

KOA
89 KOA Ln
Perryville, MO
573-547-8303
3 miles off MRT

Lodging

*Twin City Motel
450 S Truman Blvd
Crystal City, MO
636-937-7691

Super 8 Motel
1711 Hwy Z
Pevely, MO
636-475-4900

Microtel Inn
21958 Hwy 32
Ste. Genevieve, MO
573-883-8884

*Steiger Haus
242 Merchant St
Ste. Genevieve, MO
573-883-3600

Triangle Inn
897 Ste Genevieve Dr
Ste. Genevieve, MO
573-883-7191

*Budget Host Inn
221 S Kingshighway
Perryville, MO
573-547-4516

Bike Shops

*Crystal City Cyclery
2292 Truman Blvd
Crystal City, MO
636-937-6201

Mineral Area Cyclery
24 E Main St
Festus, MO
636-937-0099

Mineral Area Cyclery
9 N Jefferson St
Festus, MO
636-931-9317

Arnold to Fruitland (90 miles)

Miles N/S	Directions	Dist	S	T	Services	Miles S/N
	*Arnold				GLQR	
0	L onto US 61/67/Jeffco Rd/Commercial Blvd/Truman Blvd	13.6	4	H	GLQR	90
	*Pevely				GLQR	
	*Herculaneum				GLQR	
	*Crystal City				GLQR	
	*Festus				GLQR	
14	L onto US 61	27.9	0	M	GQ	76
42	L onto Market St (*Ste Genevieve)	1.2	0	M	GLQR	48
43	R onto Main St	0.2	0	M		47
43	L onto St Mary's Rd	0.9	0	M		47
44	L onto US 61	45.8	0	M		46
	*St Mary				Q	
	*Perryville				GLQR	
	*Fruitland		2	M	QR	
90	L onto SH 177					0

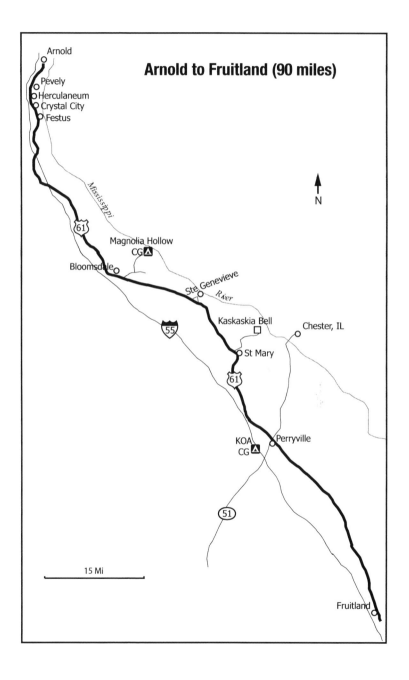

Arnold to Fruitland (90 miles)

Arnold
Pevely
Herculaneum
Crystal City
Festus

Mississippi

61

Magnolia Hollow
CG

Bloomsdale

Ste Genevieve
River

Kaskaskia Bell

Chester, IL

55

St Mary

61

N

KOA
CG

Perryville

51

15 Mi

Fruitland

Missouri: Section 4
Fruitland to Dorena (104 miles)

This final Missouri section of the MRT begins on SH 177. There is a convenience store and restaurant at the intersection of US 61 and SH 177.

Six miles from the start of this section, the MRT turns right onto CR V. SH 177 does continue straight, then links back with the county road later, but CR V has less traffic and is a more enjoyable ride. When you rejoin SH 177, the MRT continues right; however, you can turn left to ride less than a mile to reach the entrance for the Trail of Tears State Park. This is the first state park the MRT has passed in Missouri. The park is a memorial to the Cherokee Indians who lost their lives in their forced relocation during the winter of 1838–39. The Interpretative Center at the park retraces the steps of this journey through a series of interpretative panels, paintings, maps, and memorabilia. The park also includes camping.

As you approach Cape Girardeau, the MRT takes you into town on a more scenic route than SH 177 offers. The MRT turns left off of SH 177 onto Old Route V. However, there are two turns for Old Route V. Be sure to take the second turn you pass. There was an MRT sign for this turn when I rode the route. Immediately after turning onto Old Route V, the MRT veers right onto East Cape Rock Drive. This road passes through a swampy area, then climbs a hill to Cape Rock Park. This was the location where Jean Baptiste Girardot, the town's namesake, built the original trading post. The park's vista offers a breathtaking view of the MR. It is good to see the river once again.

The MRT routes cyclists through downtown Cape Girardeau. This historic district offers many attractions within walking distance, making it a good place for a break or to spend the night at a bed-and-breakfast. Two popular eating establishments located in the downtown area are Broussard's Cajun Cuisine and the "legendary" Dexter Bar-B-Que.

One of the main attractions in Cape Girardeau is its murals. Stop at the Visitors Bureau, located at 400 Broadway Avenue, to pick up a Murals of Cape Girardeau map. If you do not have time for the entire walking tour, begin your tour with the floodwall murals. This walk includes the Mississippi River Tales Mural, with 24 panels that tell the tales of Cape Girardeau and the Mississippi River; the Missouri Wall of Fame Mural, with 45 murals of persons who were born in the city and achieved fame while living in the state; and the Welcome to Cape Girardeau Mural, located on the east side of the floodwall, which traces the city's history from Native Americans through the steamboat era.

Other attractions within Cape Girardeau include Civil War sites, museums, wineries, the Bill Emerson Memorial Bridge, and much more, making it a RS. The MRT passes a variety of services on Williams Street, including Wal-Mart®, as it exits the south end of town.

Missouri Wall of Fame mural, painted on the floodwall in Cape Girardeau.

After leaving Cape Girardeau, the MRT takes cyclists on a roller-coaster ride on winding terrain through Ozark hill country. But don't despair; the flat Mississippi River Delta is not far away. These flat lands are the northernmost regions of the Mississippi alluvial plain. If you had been in this area 12,000 years ago, you would be underwater, because the Gulf of Mexico at that time extended as far north as Cape Girardeau. You will learn more about the alluvial plain as you ride through the Southern states on the MRT.

In southeast Missouri the MRT takes cyclists through rural America, past tall church steeples and farms with political banners pasted on the sides of barns. You should have no problem finding supplies and places to eat in the small towns on this part of the route, along with camping facilities.

After crossing I-57 just south of Charleston, there is a historic marker with four murals telling how the Lewis and Clark expedition camped here in preparation for their expedition. They spent five days at this site learning how to navigate the currents in the river, how to use a sexton, and other skills they would need on their voyage. There is also a marker related to the Louisiana Purchase.

After leaving the town of Charleston, cyclists will appreciate the gradual descent to the Dorena-Hickman Ferry. The route actually loses over 200 feet in elevation during the remaining 40 miles in this section. Enjoy!

The MRT passes one more RS before leaving the state of Missouri. On SH 102 there is a turn for the short ride to Big Oak Tree State Park. This preserve contains virgin hardwood forests of towering hickories and magnificent oaks, the same environment early settlers would have experienced when they first reached this "Bootheel" region of Missouri. The park's interpretative center provides educational displays explaining the history of the park. The park also includes a boardwalk that traverses the park, providing access to the unique landscape. There are five qualifying state champion tree species and two registered national champion trees within the park.

The Dorena-Hickman Ferry to Kentucky operates year-round, seven days a week, except on Christmas Day. It runs continuously on demand during daylight hours. When I last checked, the ferry was temporarily closed due to a state funding crisis. To check the status of the ferry when planning your tour, you can call 731-693-0210.

Camping

*Trail of Tears SP	Cape Camping & RV	*Boomland RV & CG
429 Moccasin Springs	1900 N Kingshighway	Hwy 105 at I-57
Jackson, MO	Cape Girardeau, MO	Charleston, MO
573-290-5268	573-332-8888	573-683-6108

Lodging

Neumeyer's B&B	*Holiday Inn	Super 8 Motel
25 Lorimier St	3253 William St	2011 N Kingshighway
Cape Girardeau, MO	Cape Girardeau, MO	Cape Girardeau, MO
573-335-0449	877-863-4780	573-339-0808
*Comfort Inn	Econo Lodge	Bell's Grade Inn
102 Drake St	310 South Story St	313 E Main St
Charleston, MO	Charleston, MO	East Prairie, MO
573-683-4200	573-683-2125	573-649-3112

Bike Shops

Cycle Werx
1407 N Kingshighway
Cape Girardeau, MO
573-334-4474

*Cape Bicycle & Fitness
2410 William St
Cape Girardeau, MO
573-335-2453

Comstock Cycle
816 Main St
Sikeston, MO
573-471-3543

Fruitland to Dorena (104 miles)

Miles N/S	Directions	Dist	S	T	Services	Miles S/N
	*Fruitland				QR	
0	L onto SH 177	6.5	2	M		104
7	R onto Route V	5.9	0	L		97
12	R onto SH 177	7.4	0	M		91
20	L onto Old Route V	0.1	0	L		84
20	Veer R remaining on E Cape Rock Dr	1.8	0	L		84
22	L onto Main St (*Cape Girardeau)	2.1	0	H	CGLQR	82
24	R onto William St/Route K	8.4	6	M		80
32	L onto SH 25 (*Gordonville)	6.8	1	M		72
39	L onto SH 77	2.9	0	M		65
42	L onto Route A (*Chaffee)	9	0	L	GQR	62
51	R onto US 61	2	2	M		53
53	L onto SH 77 (*Benton)	6.6	0	M	GQR	51
60	L onto Route D	3.6	0	L		44
63	Veer R onto Route N/Main St	10.7	0	L		41
74	S onto SH 105 (*Charleston)	9.9	6	M	GQR	30
84	L onto SH 80 (*East Prairie)	2	0	M	GQR	20
86	R onto SH 102	15.4	0	L		18
101	L onto SH 77	2.7	0	L		3
104	Dorena/HIckman Ferry (*Dorena)	0				0

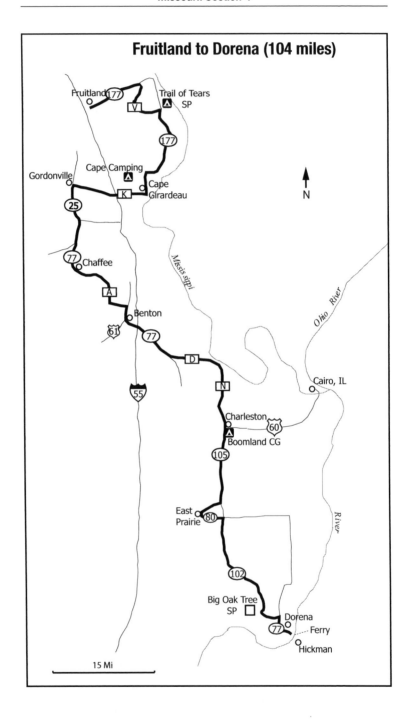

Fruitland to Dorena (104 miles)

KENTUCKY

For those cyclists riding the MRT in segments, I recommend beginning with Kentucky. The MRT just clips the western tip of the state for a total of only 61 miles. With a single day's ride you can complete one of the ten states the MRT passes through.

The ride across Kentucky is an enjoyable ride over hilly wooded countryside in the northern region and past large farm fields in the southern region. Most of the route is on rural highways with medium traffic. The MRT route is signed in Kentucky.

Kentucky: Section 1
Illinois State Line to Tennessee State Line (61 miles)

The SH 51 bridge into Kentucky is a dangerous crossing. If you are unable to arrange a police escort or hitch a ride in the back of a pickup truck, use caution during your crossing. Once you have crossed the bridge, SH 51 does have a small shoulder, but with wakeup grooves cut into the pavement, it is not a comfortable ride for cyclists.

As you enter the town of Wickliffe, you pass the entrance to Wickliffe Mounds State Historic Site. The site includes pottery, tools, bone, and shell implements excavated in the mound area. There is also a museum with exhibits about the Native Americans who occupied the mounds from AD 1100–1350. There are also restrooms and a picnic area at the site.

After leaving Wickliffe, the MRT follows rural county roads over rolling hills and through wooded forests. There are sections along this route where the tree branches form a shaded canopy over the road. The town of Columbus is located along this section of trail. As you are approaching the town, try to imagine how the area would look if the country had followed President Thomas Jefferson's proposal to move the nation's capital to Columbus. He and other national leaders felt Columbus's more central location would be a more appropriate setting for the country's capital. The proposal failed in the U.S. Senate by a single vote. It is probably best that they did not relocate the capital to Columbus. After the famous 1927 flood, the entire town was moved from the banks of the river to its present location.

The first time I rode through here there was a convenience

store in Columbus. On my most recent ride through this area the store had closed and was for sale. As I have warned before, don't take a chance that a convenience store will be open. Always carry extra food.

The turn for Belmont State Park is located in Columbus. Follow this paved road three-tenths of a mile to reach the park. There is a museum here with exhibits related to an important Civil War battle fought at the site. The massive chain and anchor that was strung across the MR by the Confederates to block Union gunboats is on display at the park. The park also has a snack-bar.

A word of warning, on both occasions I have ridden this route, at the intersection of SH 808 and SH 123, the SH 123 sign was twisted so that it appeared the road made a right turn. This is not the case; SH 123 continues straight.

South of Columbus the MRT passes a public library in the town of Hickman. Located behind the library is a community park with a covered picnic area. There is also an interesting exhibit at the park describing the history of the sheer bluff behind the library. Pause to view the bluff and read about the U.S. Army Corps of Engineers' efforts to stabilize this cliff that had been retreating at a rate of 4 to 5 feet a year.

As you continue through Hickman the MRT takes you past the Fulton County Courthouse. This is a classic turn-of-the-century Queen Anne structure with the only remaining tower in the country having an original, operating Seth Thomas clock. The Dorena-Hickman ferry entrance is located at the south end of town. You can ride the ferry across the MR to Missouri.

The MRT exits Hickman on SH 94. The road parallels the MR for several miles; however, the massive levee blocks your view of the river. Enroute to the Tennessee state line, SH 94 and SH 311 cross large, open farm fields. There is a historical marker alongside the road as you approach the border that tells an interesting story concerning a border dispute between the two states. These historical roadside markers are always a good excuse for a break.

Camping

Belmont State Park
350 Park Road
Columbus, KY
270-677-2327

Lodging

*Wickliffe Motel
520 N 4th St
Wickliffe, KY
270-335-3121

Shepherd's Inn
416 N Washington St
Clinton, KY
270-653-4212
(3 miles off MRT)

Bike Shops

Freshour Cycle Co
106 Andrea St
Sikeston, MO
573-471-3543

Illinois State Line to Tennessee State Line (61 miles)

Miles N/S	Directions	Dist	S	T	Services	Miles S/N
0	Cross Ohio River on SH 51 bridge to enter Kentucky	9.7	0	H		61
	*Wickliffe				GLQR	
10	R onto CR 1203	6.6	0	L		51
16	R at SS onto SH 123	18.8	0	M		45
	*Columbus				CR	
35	R at SS onto SH 239	6.5	0	M		26
42	R at SS onto SH 94 (*Cayce)	10.3	5	M	QR	20
	*Hickman				GQR	
52	S at SS onto Moulton St	0.2				9
52	L onto Wellington St	0.2				9
52	R at SS onto Tennessee St	0.1				9
52	L at SS onto Carroll St (1 block)	0				9
52	L at SS onto SH 94	5.5	0	M		9
58	L onto SH 311	1.7	0	L		3
60	S across CR 1282 onto SH 311	1.5	0	L		2
61	Tennessee State Line					0

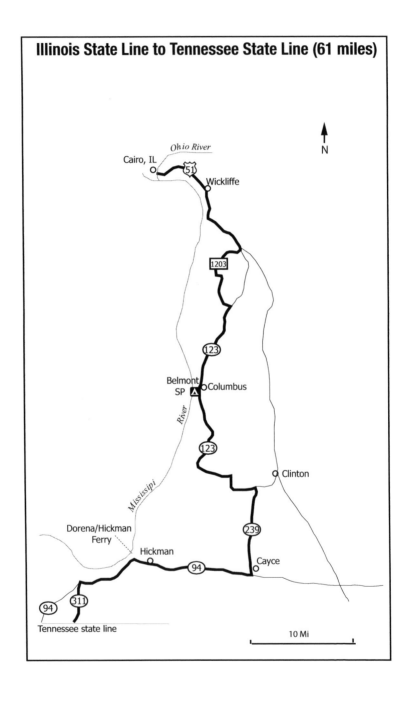

Illinois State Line to Tennessee State Line (61 miles)

TENNESSEE

Tennessee was one of the original six Southern states that began working together in 1999 to establish a trail along the Mississippi River. At that time, the organization was called the Mississippi River Hiking and Biking Corporation. Currently, all of the 168 miles of the MRT route across the state of Tennessee are signed, with the exception of the section north of Reelfoot Lake.

In its relatively short route across the state, the MRT covers a wide range of extremes. You will ride through what was the epicenter of the strongest earthquake ever recorded on the North American continent. The trail then routes cyclists through remote areas, where the narrow bluff roads are bordered by dense, lush vegetation. As its grand finale, Tennessee's MRT comes to an end in the metropolitan city of Memphis—home of the blues and the birthplace of rock 'n' roll.

Crossing the Mississippi River on the I-55 pedestrian walkway, in Memphis, Tennessee.

Tennessee: Section 1
Kentucky State Line to Cherry (86 miles)

Within 15 miles of crossing the state line, you enter the town of Samburg, which has full services. As you exit town, follow the bike route signs that direct you off of SH 22 onto a road that borders

Reelfoot Lake. Houses line the shore; however, they do not block your view of the lake.

South of Samburg, the MRT passes Reelfoot Lake State Park. This lake was formed during the 1812 New Madrid earthquake—the most severe earthquake to ever strike North America. There were reports that the earthquake was strong enough to awaken residents in Washington, D.C., and that tremors were felt as far away as Quebec City, Canada. The upheaval of the earthquake was so extreme that the MR flowed upstream. The R.C. Donaldson Memorial Museum offers exhibits and video programs related to the earthquake, and other interesting history of the area. The museum is located at the park visitor center on SH 21, 1 mile past the MRT turn onto Wynnburg Bluebank Road. There is also a raptor exhibit and a boardwalk along the lakeshore at the visitor center. This is an RS.

The state park includes campgrounds on both the north and south sides of the lake. The MRT passes the one at the south-end of the park, which is the larger of the two. This campground has showers and campsites right on the lakeshore, with giant cypress trees and views across the shallow lake. There are also primitive campsites for $8.

If your tour routes you through this area around mealtime, be sure to visit Boyette's Dining Room, located on SH 21 across the street from the park visitor center. Founded in 1912, this is one of the more renowned restaurants in Tennessee—with documented visitors from all 50 states.

After leaving the Reelfoot Lake area, you begin to see MRT signs along the route. As you ride country roads across open farmland, you will appreciate the signs as confirmation that you are on the correct road. The fields were planted in cotton during my ride through here. I have ridden on roads through cotton fields during harvest time, with drifts of cotton fiber accumulating on the road shoulder. It is entertaining to watch the fluffy cotton balls swirl about as automobiles speed by.

The long, straight stretch of road on SH 181 is an enjoyable ride. The highway is elevated as it crosses a flood plain, providing an unobstructed view across the fields and wetlands. Portions of the highway are bordered by the White Lake Refuge, and from your lofty view it is a great opportunity for viewing waterfowl. As SH 181 passes SH 104, there is a bike route sign indicating a left turn onto SH 104. This is not our route. The MRT continues straight across the intersection. However, if you don't mind a 12-mile ride, this left turn will take you to Dyersburg, which offers full services.

After leaving SH 181, you should be sure to follow the Mileage Log closely. Most of the route ahead has MRT signs; however, the route follows some very rural roads. MRT signs, and even street signs, seem to have a tendency to disappear. The first time I rode through this area, both the MRT sign and the street sign for Hobe Webb Road were missing. Within a mile past the missed turn, there was a sign for Jeff Webb Road. Hobe Webb? Jeff Webb? I reasoned that the names were so much alike that I had recorded the directions wrong. After riding around looking for a familiar sign for more miles and time than I care to admit, I backtracked to the missed turn. Riding down the road for a short distance, I passed a road sign that confirmed it was Hobe Webb Road.

Porter Gap Road offers cyclists an adventurous experience. The road borders a bluff that is covered with a massive growth of vines and kudzu. It is so lush that you almost believe you are in the tropics. It would not have been surprising to see wild orchids growing here. When there are openings in this sea of vegetation, you do have a nice view across the river bottoms.

As you reach the community of Arp, the primary MRT route turns right onto SH 19, which later becomes Crutcher Lake Road. The first time I rode the MRT through Tennessee, I followed this route. The second time I came through, I followed the alternate route. The alternate route is better signed, has better road surfaces, and is about 20 miles shorter. Therefore, I documented the alternate route in this guidebook. If you plan to camp at Fort Pillow State Historic Park, you continue for another 8 miles on SH 87 past the intersection with SH 371. You will then turn right onto Park Road to reach the campground.

This section ends in the community of Cherry. There is a convenience store that serves hot food, and it also has a covered picnic area.

Camping

*Reelfoot Lake SP
2595 SH 21
Samburg, TN
731-253-8003

Fort Pillow State Historic Park
3122 Park Road
Henning, TN
731-738-5581

Lodging

Eagle Nest Resort
P.O. Box 187
Samburg, TN
731-538-2143

Southshore Resort
P.O. Box 121
Samburg, TN
800-742-0385

Super 8 Motel
765 SH 51
Ripley, TN
731-635-8181
(4 miles off MRT)

Kentucky State Line to Cherry (86 miles)

Miles N/S	Directions	Dist	S	T	Services	Miles S/N
0	Enter Tennessee on SH 157	5.2	0	M		86
5	R ar SS onto SH 22	8.3	0	M		80
	*Samburg (Bike route to the right)				GLQR	72
14	Curve R onto SH 21	2.1	0	M		72
	*Reelfoot Lake SP				C	70
16	L onto Wynnburg Bluebank Rd	1.2	0	L		70
17	Curve R onto Owl City Rd	0.7	0	L		69
18	L onto Madie-Keefe Rd	3	0	L		68
21	Curve R at Lillie May Rd junction	1.4	0	L		65
22	R at SS onto Madie Thompson Rd	0.4	0	L		64
22	L at SS onto Madie Rd	1.3	0	L		63
24	R at SS onto Gratio Rd (no road sign)	0.5	0	L		62
24	S at SL to cross SH 78 (*Ridgely)	0.5	0	M	GQR	62
25	R at SS onto Main St (1 block)	0	0	M		61
25	L onto Depot St/Hoecake Rd	1.7	0	M		61
26	Curve L onto Levee Rd/Levee Robinson Bayou Rd/SH 79)	3.3	0	L		59
30	R at SS onto SH 181	24.7	6	M		56
	*S on SH 181 after crossing I-155					31
	*S on SH 181 after crossing SH 104 at SS					31
54	Veer R onto SH 88	6.1	0	L		31
60	R onto Porter Gap Rd (no road sign)	2.7	0	L		25
63	R at SS onto Edith Nankipoo Rd	1.6	0	L		23
65	S on Edith Nankipoo Rd	1.6	0	L		21
66	R onto Hobe Webb Rd	4.3	0	L		19
71	L at SS onto Chisholm Lake Rd	1.5	0	L		15
72	R onto Cragg School Rd	1	0	L		14
73	Veer L onto Turkey Hill Rd	1.8	0	L		13
75	L at SS onto Arp Central Rd/SH 19 (*Arp)	0.5	1	M	G	11
	*Ripley (3 miles east on SH 19)				GLQR	
75	R onto Lightfoot Luckett Rd	8.8	0	M		10
84	R onto SH 87	1.4	0	M	Q	1
86	*Cherry				Q	0

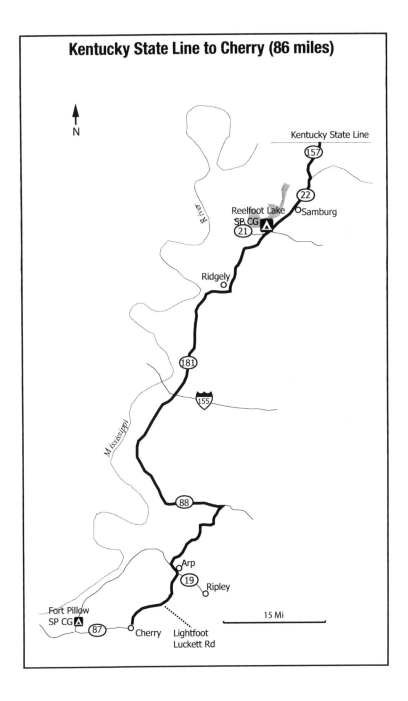

Kentucky State Line to Cherry (86 miles)

N

Kentucky State Line

157

22

Reelfoot Lake
SP CG
21
Samburg

River

Ridgely

181

155

Mississippi

88

Arp
19
Ripley

Fort Pillow
SP CG
87
Cherry
Lightfoot
Luckett Rd

15 Mi

Tennessee: Section 2
Cherry to Memphis (82 miles)

After logging so many miles on peaceful, rural country roads, it is a bit of a culture shock when you reach busy SH 151. However, there is a wide shoulder and you only ride on it for 3 miles. You also pass a rest area on SH 151, with a restroom and a picnic area. If you are in need of services, you have the option of remaining on SH 151 to reach the town of Covington, or following the MRT and entering Covington off of Simonton Road, by way of Tennessee Road. With either route, you can return to the MRT using Tennessee Road.

When you reach the junction where Detroit Road veers to the right onto Jamestown Road, you can veer left onto Giltedge Gin Road and ride 1^1/$_2$ miles to reach the Gilt Edge Café. After enjoying a fine meal, you can continue on SH 59 for less than ^{1}/$_2$ mile, then turn right onto Jamestown Road and ride another 2^1/$_2$ miles to return to the MRT. If you are riding the MRT south to north, the MRT sign at the junction of Randolph Road and Jamestown Road directs you to the café, rather than straight, which is the true MRT route.

Now the MRT begins to get serious about routing you off of the beaten path and onto narrow, twisting, hilly country roads. The farmland is replaced with dense forests and lush vegetation, which in some sections threatens to reclaim the ground the highway was built on. The route passes old, abandoned farm equipment that is overgrown with kudzu. There are even tall silos that are completely covered by the out-of-control vines. It makes for some interesting scenery along the ride. The Meeman-Shelby Forest State Park is situated in the heart of this wooded area. Located just 20 miles from Memphis, the park offers a great opportunity to freshen up before entering the city.

A mile past the Meeman-Shelby Forest State Park turnoff is the Shelby Forest General Store. Founded in 1934, the historic store has groceries, drinks, and a restaurant. Be sure to stop at the store as you pass by, even if you don't camp at the park.

I am usually apprehensive about entering large cities with the busy traffic and non-bike-friendly roads. But there is no need to be stressed about entering Memphis. With the route winding along tree-bordered country roads, then onto the Greenbelt Trail, you are not aware of the city until you are pedaling down Front Street, past the Pharaoh Ramses statue in front of the Pyramid, in downtown Memphis.

The entire downtown area is a RS. At Mud Island, you can follow the River Walk's 5-block-long scale model of the Lower Mississippi River, and visit the Mississippi River Museum. Or you can experience what Memphis is famous for, barbeque and music on Beale Street. Entire books have been written about this exciting city. I recommend that you follow the MRT to the Tennessee Welcome Center, located at 119 Riverside Drive. The helpful people at the center will assist you in collecting fliers on the area activities. With this wealth of information in hand, you could check into the Comfort Inn or Sleep Inn, both of which you passed on your ride into Memphis, and plan your visit. Either motel will put you within walking distance of a variety of entertainment spots.

When you are ready to leave Memphis, the MRT provides a pleasant send-off on the bike path that runs through Tom Lee and Martyr parks. At the end of the paved path you have two options for crossing the MR into Arkansas. The first option, which I recommend, is to push your bike on the grass-covered bank between the white-bricked Unitarian Church and the river, to a primitive path under the railroad and I-55 bridges. Once you are on the south side of both bridges, turn left up the bank to the pedestrian walkway on the I-55 bridge and ride it across the MR. The pedestrian walkway has a concrete, waist-high wall that separates you from the oncoming, southbound traffic. By the way, when you reach the top of the bank you are only a few feet from a Super 8 Motel. Also, two blocks down Alston Avenue, across from the motel, is the Mississippi River RV Park, which does allow tent camping. The second option for crossing the MR is to follow the parking lot at the end of Martyr Park out to Riverside Road, follow it right to I-55, and then ride the I-55 bridge northbound on the pedestrian walkway. After crossing the MR, continue on the shoulder another $3^1/_2$ miles to exit 3A. The first option limits you to only a short ride on the I-55 shoulder to reach the 3A exit. Read "Arkansas Section 1" in this guidebook for more details. It is unlawful to ride the interstate shoulder, but when I asked an Arkansas State Patrolman about it, he said they would ask you to take the nearest exit and they would not write you a ticket if you comply.

Camping

Meeman-Shelby Forest SP
910 Riddick Rd
Millington, TN
901-876-5215

Mississippi River RV Park
870 Cotton Gin Pl
Memphis, TN
901-946-1993

Graceland CG & Cabins
3691 Elvis Presley Blvd
Memphis, TN
866-571-9236

Lodging

*Comfort Inn Motel
901 US 51 N
Covington, TN
901-475-0380

*Sleep Inn Motel
40 N. Front St
Memphis, TN
901-522-9700

Comfort Inn Downtown
100 N. Front St
Memphis, TN
901-526-0583

Peabody Hotel
149 Union Ave
Memphis, TN
901-529-4000

Elvis Presley Heartbreak
Hotel
3677 Elvis Presley Blvd
Memphis,TN
901-332-1000

Super 8 Motel Downtown
340 W Illinois Ave
Memphis, TN
901-948-9005

Bike Shops

Midtown Bike Company
2091 Madison Ave
Memphis, TN
901-726-4511
(closest to MRT)

Peddler Bicycle Shop
575 S Highland Ave
Memphis, TN
901-327-4833

Bike Plus, Inc
7780 US Hwy 64/Stage Rd
Memphis, TN
901-385-8788

R B Cyclery Inc
8500 Wolf Lake Dr #105
Memphis, TN
901-937-4669

Cherry to Memphis (82 miles)

Miles N/S	Directions	Dist	S	T	Services	Miles S/N
	*Cherry				Q	
0	L onto SH 371	3.6	0	L		82
4	R onto Cooper Creek Rd	3.2	0	L		78
7	R at SS onto SH 51	3	5	M		75
10	R onto Leighs Chapel Rd	1.6	0	M		72
11	L onto Flat Iron Rd/Simonton Rd	4	0	M		71
	*Covington 1/2 mile to left on Tennessee Ave				GLQR	67
15	R at SS onto Murphy Rd/Bride Rd	6.1	0	L		67
22	L onto Garland Dr (*Garland)	1.4	0	L		60
23	R onto Garland Detroit Rd/Detroit Rd	6.4	0	L		59
29	Veer R onto Jamestown Rd	2.7	0	L		53
32	Veer R onto Randolph Rd	2.4	0	L		50
34	R onto Ballard Slough then L onto Needham Rd	1	0	L		48

35	R at SS onto SH 59	2.9	1	M		47
38	L onto Richardson Landing Rd	2.2	0	L		44
41	R onto Pryor Rd	2.8	0	L		41
43	L at SS onto Bluff Rd	1.8	0	L		39
45	R at SS onto Quito Drummonds Rd	0.6	0	L		37
46	R onto Ray Bluff Rd	0.2	0	L		36
46	Veer R to continue on Ray Bluff Rd	3.5	0	L		36
49	Ray Bluff Rd becomes New Bethel Rd	1.2	0	L		33
51	Curve L onto Bass Rd	0.3	0	L		31
51	R at SS onto New Bethel Rd	0.4	0	L		31
51	R at SS onto West Union Rd	1.2	0	L		31
53	R at SS onto Herring Hill Rd (no sign)	0.7	0	L		29
53	Curve L continuing on Herring Hill Rd	0.9	0	L		29
54	S on Riverbluff Rd	2.1	0	L		28
56	Continue S on Riverbluff Rd	0.7	0	L		26
57	Curve R then veer L on Bluff Rd	2.3	0	L		25
	*Meeman-Shelby Forest SP				C	23
59	R on Benjestown Rd	3.3	0	L	QR	23
63	R on Island Forty Rd	0.9	0	L		19
63	Curve L on Ramsey Rd	2.5	0	L		19
66	R at SS on Benjestown Rd	1.2	0	L		16
67	L on S Circle Rd	1.6	0	L		15
69	R at SS on Northaven	0.2	0	L		13
69	R at SS on North Watkins	1.6	3	M		13
71	R on Old Millington Rd	1.1	0	L		11
72	R on Carrolton Ave	0.7	0	L		10
72	L at SS on Benjestown Rd	1.3	0	L		10
74	R at SS on Whitney Ave/Second St	2	0	M		8
76	R on Mud Island Dr	0.6	0	L		6
76	Curve L on Island Dr (*Greenbelt Park Trail)	1.5	P	L		6
78	L on Auction Rd	0.5	S	M		4
78	R on Front St (*Memphis)	0.6	S	H	CGLQR	4
79	R on Jefferson	0.1		M		3
79	L on Bike Path in Tom Lee Park	1.8	P	L		3
81	S on river bank at end of Bike Path at Martyr's Park	0.2		L		1
81	L after primitive path under I-55 bridge	0	P	L		1
81	L up bank onto pedestrian walkway	0	P	L		1
82	Cross MR on pedestrian walkway (facing southbound traffic)	1				1
	Arkansas State Line					0

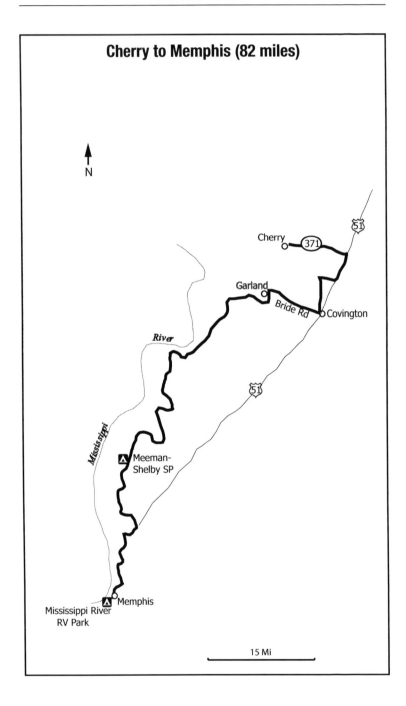

Cherry to Memphis (82 miles)

ARKANSAS

Currently the MRT in Arkansas consists of a 96-mile route from West Memphis to Helena, plus an optional, alternate route that cuts across the southeastern corner of the state. There are plans to extend the route from the state's northern border with Missouri to its southern border with Louisiana. The future extension will include the unique geological formation of Crowley's Ridge in the state's northern region and a rails-to-trails project in development across the southern area of the state.

As cyclists cross the MR into Arkansas, they have their first exposure to the southern delta region. Farming is the prominent industry in the delta, and the MRT passes through vast farmlands. Modern farming equipment has enabled landowners to work larger acreage, with fewer laborers, so the population in this area has declined since the time when manual labor was needed. This sparsely populated region provides a relaxing environment for cycling.

The MRT in Arkansas is signed, and the majority of the roads have paved shoulders. So with low traffic, paved shoulders, and hills nonexistent for the remainder of the MRT to the Gulf of Mexico, cyclists can focus on the important issues, such as where they are going to eat and sleep.

Arkansas: Section 1
West Memphis to Helena (96 miles)

The directions after crossing the I-55 bridge might seem a little puzzling, but it will make sense to you as you ride it. The route has the cyclist's safety in mind by limiting riding on busy I-55. Be sure to get an early start on this next stretch. After leaving West Memphis on SH 70, you have about an 80-mile ride before you reach a campground or motel.

Airport Road is a nice stretch to unwind on after your Memphis adventure. There is little traffic and the highway traverses what is described as "real" delta country. When you reach the end of Lake Rest Road the MRT arrow directs you to turn right, which is correct. However, there is no sign after this to direct you to turn left once you reach SH 147. So it's just a short zag to the right, then you turn left onto SH 147.

When you reach SH 131, the MRT routes you on a pleasant ride around Horseshoe Lake. If you are running short of time, you can shorten your ride by 8 miles if you stay on SH 147 and bypass the loop around the lake. Horseshoe Lake is one of the many oxbow lakes present in the lower delta region. These crescent-shaped lakes were once a part of the MR. However, over time, as the fickle river altered its course these isolated bodies of water were left behind. You will see exhibits later along the MRT that explain the process of how, as a result of natural erosion, the river developed slight curves in its course. During periods of high water, the constant force of the river ate away at the outside banks of these bends. At the same time the soil was being washed away on this outside bank, the river was depositing earth and debris on the opposite bank. This process resulted in the creation of wide sweeping turns in the river that circled around and then back to the natural corridor. Eventually, the water followed the course of least resistance and bypassed the turn completely to form a more direct route. The end result of this process was the formation of these beautiful crescent-shaped lakes that border the MR. Most of the oxbow lakes were formed 500 years ago, before man learned to tame the wild waterway with levees and constant dredging. However, later along the MRT, when you pass the Louisiana Outflow Channel, you'll discover that as late as the 1950s the river once again demonstrated it had an agenda of its own.

When you reach Marianna, those with wide tires have an optional route they can follow. To reach this route, you turn left onto SH 1B, then ride through town and follow signs to the St. Francis Ranger Station. Stop at the Ranger Station for information on Crowley's Ridge Parkway. The parkway continues past the Ranger Station through the St. Francis National Forest. The first 7 miles to Beech Point Campground are paved, but the remaining 17 miles of the parkway are gravel, until it rejoins the MRT on SH 242. This route is a nice break for cyclists who are equipped for the gravel road.

As you continue on the MRT along SH 1, if you were not following this guidebook, you would probably be unaware of your close proximity to one of the most influential landmarks in the history of the United States. This landmark is not on the MRT, but if you continue on SH 1 past the SH 242 turn, and then take a right turn on SH 49, you will be within 25 miles of Louisiana Purchase State Park. On a bicycle, a 50-mile round trip is more than a side trip. So before you start pedaling to visit this landmark, you need to know that even though it is a state park, there are no facilities. The park consists of a 950-foot boardwalk that leads you to a granite monument in the interior of a headwater swamp. Truthfully, when I first visited the site I was initially disappointed. But as I walked along the beautiful, elevated boardwalk, surrounded by the largest headwater swamp remaining in the entire Mississippi Valley, I changed my opinion. As I read the interpretive exhibits about the Louisiana Purchase, and then read the inscription on the monument itself, the reality of what this represented was overwhelming. The monument marks the initial point from which all surveys of the Louisiana Purchase territory were made. Mapping for the entire 900,000 square miles of wilderness was measured from this point. This site is important and deserves to be preserved.

Back on the MRT, after you make the turn onto SH 242, the sign that directs you to Storm Creek Lake Campground is a welcome sight for those cyclists who are camping. This is also the intersection where Crowley's Ridge Parkway rejoins the MRT, for those who chose to ride the alternate route from Marianna. It is 4.3 miles to the campground. Don't be discouraged when the pavement runs out at the boat dock and there is no campground in sight. The first time I was here, I thought the campground had been shutdown. However, even though there is no sign, at the end of the pavement continue another $1/_{10}$ mile on a hard-packed dirt road to the campground, and your reward will be camping for only $4.

The MRT follows Cherry Street through historic downtown Helena, a RS. If you are hungry, be sure to start your visit at Granny Dee's for some good home-style cooking. The town has two visitor centers, both located on Cherry Street. The Depot visitor center is housed in the old train station at the southern end of this picturesque street, and the Delta Cultural Center is only a block away. The Depot center hosts exhibits and films of the history of the river delta area. On my last visit, they were showing an interesting film about the great flood of 1927 that resulted in measures established at the national level to control the Mississippi River. The Delta Cultural Center has exhibits focusing on the roots and history of Mississippi delta music. You can also watch broadcasts of the King Biscuit Time blues radio show, which are held daily at the center on weekdays at 12:15 p.m. The center is free, but is closed on Sunday and Monday. If your ride brings you through Helena on the first weekend following Columbus Day in October, you can also attend the Arkansas Blues and Heritage Festival.

There are several motels and bed-and-breakfasts located in Helena. There are also motels located just past the turn for the SH 49 bridge, or you could stay at the Isle of Capri Casino hotel, just over the bridge in Mississippi. Maybe you'll be lucky and make enough money on the slot machines in the casino to pay for your trip. Use caution when you cross the SH 49 bridge. There is no bike lane across the long bridge, and traffic can be heavy. You might try to catch a ride across the river in the back of a pickup.

Levee wall mural in Helena, Arkansas, depicting the blues heritage of the area.

Camping

Tom Sawyer RV Park
1286 S 8th St
West Memphis, AR
870-735-9770

Storm Creek Lake CG
Ozark-St Francis Forest
4.3 miles off hwy 242
North of Helena, AR

Lodging

New Hampshire Inn
898 Ingram Blvd
West Memphis, AR
870-733-1780

Holiday Inn I-55
I-55/I-40 & Ingram Blvd
West Memphis, AR
870-735-4055

Downtown Inn
416 Walnut St
Helena, AR
870-338-6908

*Edwardian Inn B&B
317 Biscoe St
Helena, AR
870-338-9155

Super 7 Motel
1007 Martin Luther King Dr
Helena, AR
870-753-9701

Isle of Capri Casino
777 Isle of Capri Pkwy
Lula, MS
662-363-2250

Bike Shops

N/A

West Memphis to Helena (96 miles)

Miles N/S	Directions	Dist	S	T	Services	Miles S/N
0	At end of I-55 pedestrian walkway, walk your bike down southside shoulder then turn R on Dacus Lake Rd	0.6	0	L		96
1	R onto Bridgeport Rd (ride under I-55)	0.3	0	L		96
1	Curve L paralleling I-55 (northside of the interstate)	0.9	0	L		95
2	At end of road push bike up embankment then R on I-55	0.8	8	X		95
3	Exit at 3A for SH 131	0.1	0	X		94
3	R at SS to curve under I-55	1	4	L		94
4	L onto US 70 (*West Memphis)	2.3	0	H	GLQR	93
	*L turn to Tom Sawyer CG (8 miles)		0	M	C	
6	L at SL onto Airport Rd/Waverly Rd/Lake Rest Rd	10.8	0	L	G	90
17	At SS zag R then L onto SH 147	9.9	8	M		80
27	L onto SH 131	8.8	0	L	G	70
36	S onto SH 147	2.6	0	M		61
38	L at SS onto SH 38	7.7	3	L	GQR	58
46	L onto US 79 (*Hughes)	20.9	5	M	QR	51
67	L at SL onto SH 1 (*Marianna)	12.5	5	M	GQR	30
79	L onto SH 242	9.5	3	L	CQ	17
	* L onto CR 217 to Storm Cr Lake CG (4.3 miles)		0	L		
89	L on Anderson St	0.4	0	L		8
89	S at SS onto Springdale Rd	2.8	0	L		7
92	S at SS onto College St	0.3	0	L		4
92	L onto Market St	0.5	0	L		4
93	R at SS onto Cherry St (*Helena)	0.6	0	L	GLQR	4
93	R onto Missouri St	0.3	0	L		3
94	L at SS onto Columbia St/Biscoe St	1.6	0	M	L	3
95	L at SL onto US 49 to bridge	1.1	0	X		1
96	Mississippi State Line					0

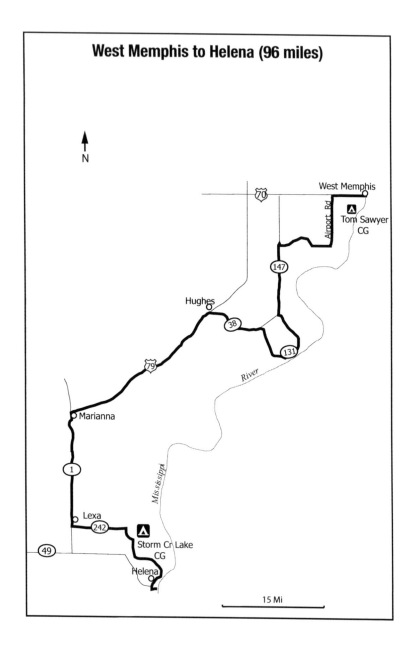

West Memphis to Helena (96 miles)

N

West Memphis

Tom Sawyer CG

Airport Rd

70

147

Hughes

38

131

79

River

Marianna

1

Lexa

242

49

Storm Cr Lake CG

Mississippi

Helena

15 Mi

Arkansas: Alternate Route
Greenville, MS, to Vicksburg, MS (95 Miles)

The main route of the MRT continues south, through the state of Mississippi. This alternate route crosses the MR into Arkansas, cuts across the southeastern corner of the state, and then enters the northeastern corner of Louisiana. If you combine this route with the eastern route of the MRT through Mississippi, it would make a good 200-mile loop tour. Loops are great, because they don't require a shuttle. The alternate route begins south of Greenville, Mississippi. To reach the start of the alternate route, exit Greenville using the directions documented in "Mississippi Section 2" of this guidebook. When you reach the intersection with SH 454, turn right onto SH 454, rather than continuing across the intersection on Main Extended.

When I rode this route, I had to use the old US 82 bridge across the MR. This is a very dangerous crossing. The bridge is narrow and traffic is heavy. This is another crossing where I advise cyclists to catch a ride in the back of a pickup truck. There is a new bridge under construction, with a scheduled completion date in the spring of 2009. The bridge will provide a biker-friendly crossing with wide shoulders. The new bridge will also be the longest cable-stayed bridge on the MR. The main span of the bridge was completed when I rode this route, and it is truly an impressive feat of engineering.

The MRT passes the Harlow Casino prior to crossing the river into Arkansas. Along with gambling, the casino offers rooms and a restaurant. After crossing the bridge, cyclists can turn right and follow signs to reach camping at the Chicot County RV Park. This is a nice, commercial campground right on Chicot Lake, about 4$^{1}/_{2}$ miles off the MRT. Chicot Lake is also North America's largest oxbow lake.

Through this southern corner of Arkansas, the MRT follows US 65, which has a wide shoulder and is bordered by flat farmland. You ride past complex irrigation ditches in rice fields through this area, as well as soybean fields, cotton fields, and even a few catfish farms. Arkansas is the number-one rice producer in the United States. Initially, farmers in the area had a difficult time accepting the concept of flooding their fields to grow grain. But judging by the numerous irrigation channels crisscrossing the rice fields, it looks like the farmers adjusted to the process.

As it enters Lake Providence, the MRT borders the lake, giving cyclists scenic views of cypress trees on both lakeshores. There are several points of interest along this stretch to visit, including the Byerley House—that serves as a visitor center—, the Louisiana State Cotton Museum, Grant's Canal Park, and a 600-foot lake pier.

As you continue south on US 65, the giant bat painted on a water tower signals your arrival at Transylvania. Stop at the convenience store to pick up a souvenir T-shirt to commemorate your visit to the town, and that you survived your visit. There is a sign at the store greeting visitors with, "Welcome to Transylvania. We're always looking for new blood."

The long stretch of the MRT on US 65 is a pretty nice ride. The road maintains a wide shoulder the entire distance, and there are enough eating places along the route that a cyclist could gain weight riding this section. As you reach Tallulah and turn onto US 80, there is no shoulder, but traffic is low on this road. This road passes the location of the first indoor shopping mall in the United States. The building remains, but the mall is no longer open. US 80 also passes another memorial to Grant's Canal. There were four attempts to dig canals in an effort to bypass the Confederate guns positioned on the bluffs of Vicksburg. Most of these canals have been destroyed by farming operations, but a small segment of one of these canals remains at this memorial site, preserving the original width and depth of the man-made channel.

The southern section of this alternate route concludes when CR 3218 reaches the river. There are plans to open the old CR 3218 bridge across the MR to pedestrians and bicycles; however, at this time you cannot cross the bridge without the permission of the Vicksburg Bridge Commission. Cyclists will need to call the commission at 601-636-0881 a day or more ahead of their arrival to get permission to cross the bridge. Someone from the Vicksburg Bridge Commission will then haul you across the bridge in their truck on weekdays between 8 a.m. and 5 p.m. When you reach the bridge on the Louisiana side, the Delta City Town Hall, located next to the bridge, might allow you use their phone to notify the Vicksburg Bridge Commission of your arrival.

Once across the bridge, follow the paved road up a little knoll to reach the Mississippi Welcome Center. You can then rejoin the MRT as described in "Mississippi Section 3" of this guidebook.

Camping

Warfield Point Park
295 Warfield Point Park Rd
Greenville, MS
662-335-7275

Chicot County Park RV
Street 819 Lakehall Rd
Lake Village, AR
870-265-3500

*Lakeview Inn & RV
7232 Hwy 65 North
Lake Providence, LA
318-559-5253

Lodging

*Pines Motel
2151 Highway 65
Eudora, AR
870-355-5555

*Economy Inn
9634 Highway 65 South
Lake Providence, LA
318-559-3801

Days Inn
143 Highway 65 South
Tallulah, LA
318-574-5200

Bike Shops

N/A

Greenville, MS, to Vicksburg, MS (95 Miles)

Miles N/s	Directions	Dist	S	T	Services	Miles S/N
	*Greenville, MS					
0	R at intersection of Main Extended and SH 454	4.4	0	M		95
	*R-off MRT-onto US 82 to Warfield Point Park (3 miles)	0	0	M	C	
4	L on US 82 to cross the MR	8.6	1	H	CR	91
	*R-off MRT-after exiting bridge to Chicot County RV Park (4.2 miles)		0	L	C	
13	L on US 65	63.8	8	M	CGLQR	82
	*Eudora				GLQR	
	*Lake Providence				CGLQR	
	*Transylvania					
77	L on US 80 (*Tallulah)	14.4	0	L	GLQR	18
91	S on CR 3218	2.2	0	L		4
93	S cross MR on CR 3218 bridge	1.6	P			2
95	*Vicksburg, MS				GLQR	0

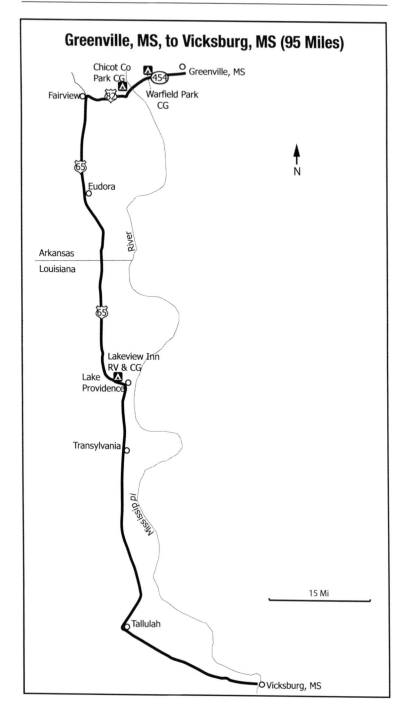

Greenville, MS, to Vicksburg, MS (95 Miles)

Chicot Co Park CG

Greenville, MS

454

Fairview

82

Warfield Park CG

N

65

Eudora

River

Arkansas

Louisiana

65

Lakeview Inn RV & CG

Lake Providence

Transylvania

Mississippi

15 Mi

Tallulah

Vicksburg, MS

MISSISSIPPI

The Arkansas MRT gave you an introduction to the southern delta region, and now the Mississippi MRT takes you through the heart of the southern delta region. You only thought you were in flat country as you rode across Arkansas. If you look up the word "flat" in the dictionary, it should read "See Mississippi delta."

This area is celebrated as the birthplace of the blues. A short side trip from the MRT will take you to US 61, known as the "Blues Highway." The MRT passes through areas where blues legends such as Muddy Waters, Robert Johnson, and Robert Nighthawk lived and performed.

Control of the Mississippi River was of vital importance during the Civil War. There were many major battles fought in this region that directly affected the final outcome of the war. As you follow the MRT through Vicksburg and Natchez, you will have many opportunities to learn more about these conflicts.

The 302 miles of the MRT in Mississippi are signed. However, you should keep the Mileage Log handy. I became totally disoriented as I was leaving Vicksburg, circling completely back around to the downtown area, even though the route was well posted with MRT signs. The problem was that someone had either posted the turn arrow incorrectly, or someone had changed it. I blindly followed the arrow right, when I should have known from my directions that the MRT turned left. The golden rule of touring is to know your route.

Mississippi: Section 1
Arkansas State Line to Greenville (103 miles)

Use caution when you ride the 7 miles on US 49, after you cross the MR into Mississippi. This is a narrow highway, with a gravel shoulder, and traffic is often heavy. When I rode this route, there were two different streets signed as Lula-Moon Lake Road. My map shows the second road should be Moon Lake Road. The MRT follows the second road. There is also a brown sign for Moon Lake at this turn. I don't believe you'll be tempted to take the first road, because it's gravel.

Moon Lake is another crescent-shaped oxbow lake. The MRT borders the lakeshore. As you ride along the lake, you will pass an inn and restaurant named Uncle Henry's Place. During Prohibition, this was one of the South's most famous speakeasies. The club had fresh Maine lobsters and Kansas City steaks flown in for its clientele. As a child, Tennessee Williams frequented the club with his grandfather, and the club appeared in a number of his dramas as Moon Lake Casino. Today, the setting is a mere shell of what it once was. However, if you use your imagination, you can visualize what Uncle Henry's Place might have been like during its heyday in the 1930s. Shiny new automobiles, filled with sharply dressed passengers, speed along Moon Lake Road. As they arrive at Uncle Henry's and the party-goers climb out of the vehicles, laughing and joking, a man wearing a tuxedo greets them. As he opens the front door of Uncle Henry's Place, loud music pours out into the dark night. If only the walls of Uncle Henry's Place could talk, what stories they would tell.

Farther along on the MRT, you'll reach another historic landmark in the town of Friars Point. Stop outside Hirsberg's Drug Store to read the Mississippi Blues Trail marker about famous bluesman Robert Nighthawk, who called Friars Point his home. He and Robert Johnson used to play on the drug store's front steps. A few miles farther south on SH 1, is the Stovall Plantation, birthplace of Muddy Waters. Take a short side trip off of SH 1 to Clarksdale, where you can see the famous crossroads intersection where bluesman Robert Johnson allegedly sold his soul to the devil in exchange for fame. This delta area was home to many legendary blues musicians. It would have been great to have ridden along these roads during that era, passing small homes with musicians sitting on front porches, playing music for the pure pleasure of it.

For the next 70 miles on SH 1, you'll be riding past wide-open farmland. Years ago these roads were lined with shotgun shacks, where the people who worked these fields lived. Today large corporations operate many of these farms. With their huge tractors and farm equipment, they can work the fields using only a handful of workers.

About a mile before you reach the Great River Road State Park, you will ride through the town of Rosedale, which has a grocery store and a restaurant. In the park there is a concession stand, a disc golf course, a playground, and a campground with showers. There is also a 75-foot tower that gives you a great view of the MR and its sandy banks.

As you leave Rosedale, SH 1 picks up a 2-foot shoulder. If you come through this area during the autumn harvest, you'll see drifts of cotton along the roadside. As vehicles drive past you, the balls of white cotton swirl around on the pavement like dry fluffy snowflakes. Also after the harvest, the fresh-cut fields are filled with thousands of birds feeding on newly exposed insects, seeds, and worms.

About twenty miles down the road, there is a restaurant located in the town of Scott. The restaurant is not on SH 1. To reach it, turn left at the sign for the D&PL truck entrance. A little farther south on SH 1, you'll pass the Winterville Mounds State Park and Museum, a RS. The mounds were built in 1000 A.D. There are twelve mounds remaining at the site, including the 55-foot-high Temple Mound, which offers a great view of the flat delta farmland. It is a very interesting stop and admission is free. The Native American Days festival is held at the site each year in early November. The festival hosts Native American groups from all across the nation.

Greenville offers full services for cyclists, as well as, historic exhibits, plantation homes, walking tours, museums, and numerous other attractions. If you are planning to tour the area, I recommend that you stop at the Washington County Convention and Visitors Bureau, located at 216 S Walnut Street. Their phone number is 662-334-2711. They can provide you with maps and fliers to help you plan your visit. You can reach the visitors bureau by following the MRT to the intersection of Broadway and Main streets, and rather than turning left as instructed, take a right turn. Follow Main Street for 4 blocks, then turn left onto Walnut Street. There are hotels and restaurants in the vicinity of the visitors bureau, and if you're ready to camp, Warfield Point Park is located about 3 miles away.

Camping

*Great River Road SP
Rosedale, MS
662-759-6762
(1.4 miles off SH 1)

Warfield Point Park
295 Warfield Point Park Rd
Greenville, MS
662-335-7275

Lodging

*Uncle Henry's Place
5860 Moon Lake Road
Dundee, MS
662-337-2757

*Isle of Capri Casino
777 Isle of Capri Parkway
Lula, MS
800-843-4753

Greenville Inn & Suites
211 S Walnut St
Greenville, MS
622-332-6900

Fairfield Inn
137 N. Walnut St
Greenville, MS
662-332-0508

Bike Shops

Kwik Keys & Bikes
902 Hwy 82 East
Greenville, MS
662-335-5987

Arkansas State Line to Greenville (103 miles)

Miles N/S	Directions	Dist	S	T	Services	Miles S/N
0	Enter MS on US 49 bridge	6.9	0	H	LQR	103
7	R onto Moon Lake Rd	6.7	0	L	LR	96
14	L at SS onto SH 1	0.7	0	M		90
14	R onto Seep Water Rd/2nd St	4.6	0	L		89
19	L onto James Washington Sr Dr (*Friars Point)	0.1	0	L		84
19	R onto Oak St/Oakridge Rd/McKee Rd	4.7	0	L		84
24	R at SS onto SH 1	77.3	0	M		80
31	*L onto SH 322 to Clarksdale (8 miles)				GLQR	2
	*Rosedale				GQR	2
65	*R onto St Park Rd (*Great River Road SP 1.4 miles)				C	2
94	*Winterville Mounds SP					2
101	R at SL onto Broadway St	2.3	6	H		2
	*Greenville				GLQR	0
103	L onto Main St/Main Extended					0

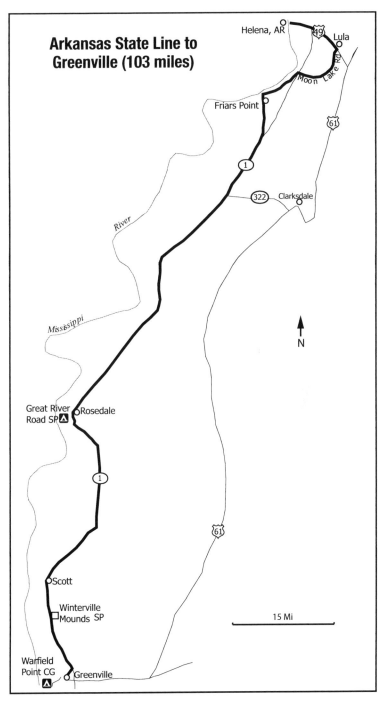

Arkansas State Line to Greenville (103 miles)

Helena, AR

Lula

Moon Lake Rd

61

Friars Point

1

322 Clarksdale

River

Mississippi

N

Great River Road SP ⚑ Rosedale

1

61

Scott

Winterville Mounds SP

15 Mi

Warfield Point CG ⚑ Greenville

Mississippi: Section 2
Greenville to Vicksburg (111 miles)

Approximately 6 miles south of Greenville, you will cross SH 454. If you choose to ride the "Arkansas Alternate Route" included in this guidebook, you will turn right on SH 454. This alternate route takes cyclists across the southeastern corner of Arkansas and the northeastern corner of Louisiana. It then rejoins the Mississippi MRT route in Vicksburg, Mississippi. If you choose to remain on the Mississippi MRT, continue straight across the SH 454 intersection, on Main Extended.

The MRT returns to SH 1 once again; however, you won't be on it for such a long distance like you were north of Greenville. You will turn off SH 1 onto Roy's Store Road. And you'll never guess where this road takes you. To Roy's Store! If a store is worth having a highway named after it, you have to make it a RS. This novel place is truly like stepping back in time. It is an old store that is a combination gas station, grocery, and diner. I loved the tractor seats mounted on the stools at the soda counter. Roy's Store also has a campground and cabins, in case you want to hang out with the locals on the porch. Seriously, you will enjoy the friendly people here, and the good food.

The ride around Lake Washington is a pleasant experience. As you leisurely pedal along the shore, watch for waterfowl on the lake. You pass the remains of the St. John Protestant Episcopal Church founded in 1854. Be sure to stop and read the historical marker.

As the MRT runs along SH 465, it gives cyclists a nice treat. It routes you right on top of the levee for about 12 miles. The large fields you have been riding past the last two days have been replaced by dense woods and wetlands. This area is open range, so watch for the rough cattle guards on the road. Chotard Landing is located right off the levee, on the shores of Chotard Lake. It has a campground, a small grocery, and a nice family tavern with pool tables, dart games, and a dance floor. In the evening, the owners fire up the barbecue and grill food for their guests. If you're not ready to stop, there is a restaurant and a convenience store another 10 miles farther south on the MRT, and just past that, there is camping at the Sunset View Resort.

Use caution when crossing the bridge over the Yazoo River on US 61. Traffic can be pretty heavy here. After World War I, US 61 was known as the "Great Migration" path for the mass exodus of over five million black sharecroppers, who relocated to the industrialized Northern states.

The ruins of St. John Protestant Episcopal Church, founded in 1854. The lead from the window frames was used for bullets during the Civil War.

There is heavy truck traffic on Old Highway 61. There isn't a shoulder on the road, so keep watch in your mirror. Most of the trucks will turn off at the Port of Vicksburg. As you watch the traffic, also keep an eye out for Margaret's Grocery. Words can't describe this unique folk-art structure. You'll have to see it for yourself.

Vicksburg is a paradise for anyone interested in history, especially Civil War history. Memorials line the streets documenting the vital role the area played in the "War Between the States." Vicksburg was a strategic location during the war, with many momentum-shifting conflicts staged in the area. This is definitely a RS. If you continue on Washington Street another 2.7 miles past the MRT turn onto Veto Street, you will reach the Mississippi Welcome Center. They have a wealth of information on the attractions in the area to help you plan your visit. Be sure to pick up brochures for the Red and Blue Scenic Tours. There are also hotels and casinos in the vicinity of the center, providing you another opportunity to pay for your trip.

From the view of the MR at the Welcome Center, you can see the old CR 3218 bridge off to your right. If you had taken the Arkansas Alternate Route after leaving Greenville, this is the bridge you would have crossed to return to the MRT. The bridge is currently closed, but if you phone the Vicksburg Bridge Commission in advance, at 601-636-0881, they will transport you across the bridge at no charge. If you combine the Arkansas Alternate Route with the Mississippi MRT, it makes a great 200-mile loop tour between Vicksburg and Greenville.

Camping

*Roy's Store Cabins & CG
7 Roy's Store Road
Chatham, MS
662-827-2588

*Chotard Landing
Hwy 465
Vicksburg, MS
601-279-4282
(campground & cabins)

*Sunset View Resort
14640 Highway 465
Vicksburg, MS
601-279-4723
(campground & motel)

Lodging

Annabelle B&B Inn
501 Speed St
Vicksburg, MS
800-791-2000

*Dixiana Motel
4041 Washington St
Vicksburg, MS
601-631-6940

*La Quinta Inn
4216 Washington St
Vicksburg, MS
800-531-5900

Bike Shops

N/A

Greenville to Vicksburg (111 miles)

Miles N/S	Directions	Dist	S	T	Services	Miles S/N
	*Greenville					
0	L onto Main St/Main Extended	8.1	0	M	GR	111
	*R on SH 454 for AR Alternate Route		0	M		
8	L at SS on Wilmont St	0.3	0	L		103
8	R at SS on SH 1	12.7	2	M	Q	103
	*L onto SH 12 to Leroy Percy SP (8 miles)		0	L	C	
21	R on Roy's Store Rd	1.3			CGLR	90.2
22	L on East Lake Washington Rd	9.4	0	L	GQ	88.9
32	L on Cordell Rd	0.5	0	L		79.5
32	R at SS on Glenallen Rd (no street sign)	7.2	0	L		79
40	R at SS SH 1	19.6	0	L		71.8
	*Mayersville				QR	
59	R on SH 465	39.3	0	L	CQR	52.2
	*Chotard Landing				CQR	
	*Sunset View Resort				C	
98	R at SS on US 61	5.3	0	H		12.9
104	R onto Port of Vicksburg Rd/Old US 61/Washington St	7.6	0	H	R	8
111	L at SS onto Veto St (*Vicksburg)				CGLQR	0

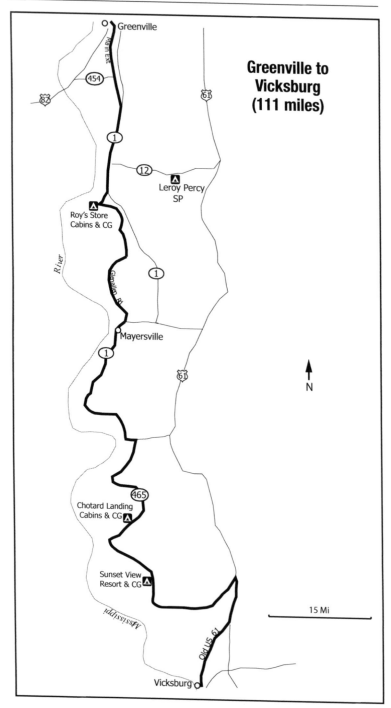

Greenville

454

82

1

12

Leroy Percy SP

Roy's Store Cabins & CG

River

Glenallan Rd

1

Mayersville

1

61

465

Chotard Landing Cabins & CG

Sunset View Resort & CG

Mississippi

Old US 61

Vicksburg

Greenville to Vicksburg (111 miles)

N

15 Mi

Mississippi: Section 3
Vicksburg to Natchez (88 miles)

The MRT routes you out of Vicksburg on narrow winding roads. Initially, the traffic is heavy, but after a few miles the number of vehicles lessens, and it becomes a pleasant ride. About 14 miles out of town at the Old Port Gibson Road intersection, you pass the old Crossroads Store. This is an interesting place to stop for a cool drink and a snack.

Cyclists get a bonus as the MRT includes a portion of the Natchez Trace Parkway on the route. The entire parkway is 444 miles long, extending from Natchez, Mississippi, to Nashville, Tennessee. The trail, originally used by Native Americans, was well enough established that it was included in the earliest maps by the French in 1733. The Old Trace is best known as the return route used by farmers from the Ohio River region, after they floated their crops down river to Natchez and New Orleans. With the strong river current, returning by boat was not an option. When these "Kaintucks" reached their destination, they sold their flatboats for lumber and began their trek back by the most direct route. Already an established route, the trace became the most heavily traveled road in the Southwest during the early 1800s. At its peak, before river steamboats became the most popular means of travel, there were more than 20 inns along the trace that catered to the needs of these travelers. The MRT passes Mount Locust Inn and Plantation, the only inn remaining on the route. With its smooth blacktop surface, bordered by tall moss-covered trees, the trace continues to be a popular route for travelers of the two-wheel variety.

Shortly after merging onto the Natchez Trace Parkway, you will pass Rocky Springs Campground. There is a hiking trail from the campground that will take you to the old Rocky Springs town site. As you walk among the sparse remains of the town site, it is difficult to imagine that in 1860 this was a prosperous community with a population of almost 3,000 people. The town was unable to rebuild after the devastation it suffered during the Civil War.

The Mileage Log lists an optional side trip to Port Gibson, referred to by General Grant as "the town too pretty to burn." The town offers cyclists full services. For those wishing to camp, Natchez State Park is another 30-mile ride on the MRT. If you are a Civil War buff, there is another optional trip 8 miles northwest of Port Gibson to Grand Gulf Military Monument Park. The park includes two forts, a cemetery, a museum, a campground, hiking trails, several restored buildings, and an observation tower. To reach the park, follow Grand Gulf Road out of Port Gibson.

After a restful night at either Port Gibson or Natchez State Park, and you are once again back on the MRT, you will pass Emerald Mound Site, a RS. Park your bike and walk to the top of the second-largest temple mound in the United States. The leveled area on top of the mound is as large as a soccer field. It could accommodate over a hundred Native American worshipers, as they performed their dancing rituals and sang their songs of prayer. As you stand on top of the mound, try to imagine what one of these religious ceremonies would have been like. It must have been a spiritually motivating and uplifting experience.

I know I sound like a broken record, but in Natchez, your first stop should be the Natchez Visitor Reception Center. The MRT runs right past it, and the center has a dedicated staff whose primary job is to assist you in planning a tour to meet your interests. I also recommend that you view the video at the visitor center. The background information it provides will make your tour all the more interesting. If you schedule your visit in March or April, you can experience the Spring Pilgrimage, a cherished Southern tradition for over 70 years. During the pilgrimage, over 30 historic houses open their doors for tours, with hostesses dressed in period costumes. Prior to the Civil War, over half of the millionaires in the United States lived in Natchez, and many of their plantations, antebellum mansions and Victorian-era townhouses now operate as bed-and-breakfasts. So if you are a little burnt out with camping, and would like to reward yourself by staying in a bed-and-breakfast, this would be a great city to do it in. At the end of your day touring this fascinating city—definitely a RS—you could sit on the patio of Fat Mama's Tamales to enjoy their signature dish, and then wash it down with their famous "Knock-You-Naked" margaritas.

After your visit in Natchez, continue on Canal Street past the visitor center, to cross the MR on the US 65 bridge. There are two northbound lanes on the bridge, but no shoulder. Traffic can be heavy at times, so use caution.

Camping

River Town CG
5900 Hwy 61 S
Vicksburg, MS
866-442-2267
(5 miles south of town)

*Rocky Springs CG
5 miles on Natchez Trace
Pkwy
Rocky Springs, MS

*Natchez State Park
230 Wickcliff Road
Natchez, MS
601-442-2658

Lodging

Bernheimer House
212 Walnut St
Port Gibson, MS
601-437-2843

Grand Gulf Inn
2017 Hwy 61 N
Port Gibson, MS
601-437-8811

Oak Square Plantation
1207 Church St
Port Gibson, MS
601-437-5300

B&B reservations
for over 40 residences
Natchez, MS
(800-647-6742)

Hampton Inn
627 Canal Street
Natchez, MS
601-446-6770

Isle of Capri Casino & Hotel
70 Silver St
Natchez, MS
601-445-0605

Bike Shops

Trippe's Western Auto
180 Sgt Prentiss Dr
Natchez, MS
601-446-5273

Emerald Mound Site, near Natchez, Mississippi, is one of the largest ceremonial mounds in North America.

Vicksburg to Natchez (88 miles)

MS Miles	Directions	Dist	S	T	Services	Miles S/N
	*Vicksburg				GLQR	
0	L at SS onto Veto St	0.2	0	H		88
0	R onto Monroe St/Drummond St	0.6	0	H		88
1	L at SS onto Harris St	0.1	0	H		88
1	L at SL onto Cherry St	0.1	0	H		88
1	R onto Chambers St	0.4	0	H		87
1	L at SS onto Glenwood Circle	0.1	0	H		87
2	Curve L onto Vicklan St (no steet sign)	0.1	0	H		87
2	R at SS onto Macarthur Dr	0.2	0	H		87
2	R at SL onto Mission 66/Confederate Ave	0.6	0	H		87
2	L at SL onto Indiana Ave	1	0	H		86
3	R at SS onto Porters Chapel Rd	2.9	0	H		85
6	R at SS onto Halls Ferry Rd	1.5	0	H		82
8	L at SS onto Fisher Ferry Rd	14.9	0	M	GQ	81
23	R onto Natchez Trace Pkwy	48.8	0	M		66
	*Rocky Springs CG				C	
	*R to Port Gibson (2 miles)		0	M	GLQR	
72	R onto SH 553(*L on SH 553 to Natchez SP 2.6 miles)	0.1	0	M	C	17
72	L onto Emerald Mound Rd	1.9	0	L		17
74	R at SS onto McGehee Rd	0.9	0	L		15
74	L at SS onto Artman Rd	1.7	0	L		14
76	R at SS onto Airport Rd	3.7	0	L		12
80	L at SS onto Martin Luther King Jr St	6.7	0	M	GQR	9
87	R at SL onto Main St	0.4	0	M	R	2
87	L at SL onto Canal St	0.8	0	M	GLR	2
	*Natchez Visitor Reception Center				GLQR	
88	R at SL onto US 65 bridge	0.7	0	X		1
88	*Louisiana					0

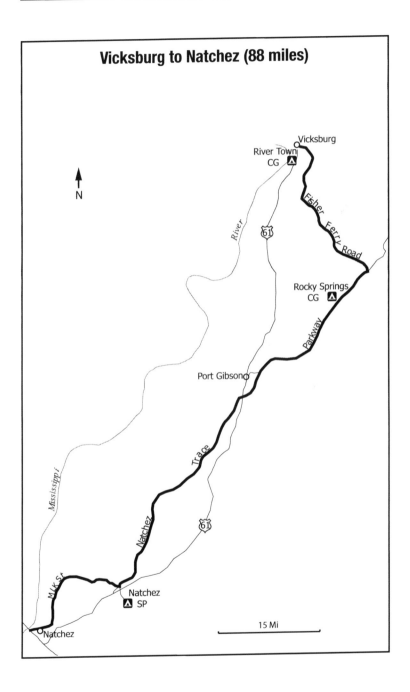

Vicksburg to Natchez (88 miles)

Vicksburg

River Town CG

N

River

61

Fisher Ferry Road

Rocky Springs CG

Parkway

Port Gibson

Trace

61

Natchez

Mississippi

Natchez Trace

Mlk Sf

Natchez SP

Natchez

15 Mi

LOUISIANA

For those cyclists who began the MRT in Minnesota, this is the final leg of your journey. You have another 349 miles to ride, and then you can contact Mississippi River Trail, Inc., to request your official certificate of completion. It has been a fantastic ride across the country, and the ride through Louisiana is a great ending to the route.

The Louisiana MRT begins with a beautiful ride along a levee road that offers great wildlife viewing opportunities in the surrounding wetlands. Farther south, it routes you past beautiful ante-bellum homes. Unlike the mansions in Vicksburg and Natchez, Mississippi, these homes are set on large plantations. You could almost imagine Scarlett O'Hara sitting in front of one of these elegant homes, in the shade of a giant oak tree, sipping on a mint julep.

The MRT tops off the adventure by routing cyclists through the heart of the Queen City of the South, New Orleans. What can I say about the Big Easy? If you've been there before, you need no encouragement to return to the city, and if you haven't been there before, you are in for a treat.

The Louisiana MRT is not signed at this time. Most of the route across the state follows rural roads, with traffic rated low or medium. The only elevation gain you will experience is when the MRT climbs the levee bank.

Louisiana: Section 1
Vidalia to Livonia (104 miles)

You cross the MR into Louisiana at the town of Vidalia. If you are in need of supplies, there is a grocery store located on US 65, 2 miles past the turn for SH 131. It is over 60 miles before you reach another grocery store. Just outside of Vidalia, the MRT passes the River View RV Park & Resort. Other than primitive campsites, River View RV Park and Deer Park Lake Campground are the only campgrounds until you reach Morganza, 70 miles away. For cyclists staying at commercial lodging, Vidalia has the last motel until you reach New Roads, which is 20 miles past Morganza.

It's hard to beat the 46-mile ride on SH 15. With a paved shoulder, medium traffic, and a ride either on top of the levee or alongside it, you can attain a cycling Zen. The miles of wetlands bordering the highway offer incredible opportunities for viewing wildlife. I saw an enormous flock of pelicans in this area. The MRT passes an old visitor center operated by Louisiana Hydroelectric. But don't bother to call the phone number listed on the door to request a tour, because they no longer provide tours. However, if you continue on the MRT to the auxiliary dam office, the U.S. Corps of Engineers naturalist will explain the fascinating story behind the purpose of the structures you are passing. The auxiliary dam and old river lock are manned 24 hours a day. You can press the call button at the gate to contact them. For a tour of the facility you can stop by unannounced, and take a chance that the naturalist is available, or you can call 225-492-2169 to schedule a visit. The U.S. Corps of Engineers facility also provides a much-needed water stop on this empty stretch of road.

The interesting history behind these structures makes this a RS. These dams and control facilities built along SH 15 are another example of man's ongoing attempt to control the MR. For centuries, the Red River has run parallel to the MR in this area. Farther south, the Red River flows into the Atchafalaya River and on to Morgan City, where it empties into the Gulf of Mexico, while the MR flows through New Orleans on its way to the Gulf of Mexico. The MR, when it was an untamed waterway, developed an exaggerated bend that resulted in it crossing channels with the Red River. When the two rivers merged, the Red River began flowing into the MR. Without the water from the Red River, the Atchafalaya River became clogged with logs and debris. In 1839, local citizens began the mammoth task of clearing out the huge logjam that blocked the Atchafalaya River. Once opened, not only did the Atchafalaya resume channeling the waters of the Red River, but also ten percent of the MR was redirected into it. By 1920 over twenty percent of the water from the MR was flowing into the Atchafalaya River. In 1950, the flow of water from the MR had grown to thirty percent. The U.S. Corps of Engineers concluded that within a few decades the Atchafalaya River, with its shorter, more direct route to the Gulf, would become the main channel for the MR. This would be a disaster for the shipping ports in Baton Rouge and New Orleans. The naturalist can explain how these facilities operate to control this battle with nature.

Be sure to top off your water supply at the U.S. Corps of Engineers facility, especially, if you plan to camp at one of the primitive campsites. The MRT passes two primitive campgrounds at about mile 52 in this section's Mileage Log. They are both located just off the right side of the levee. I recommend the second of the campsites, just before the bridge across the old river lock.

179

As you ride on SH 420, you will pass the first of what will be many stretches of Louisiana roadways lined by huge, century-old live oak trees. Live oaks were often planted to frame the entrance to large plantation homes. Many of the homes have been destroyed, but the trees live on as a monument to that era of American history.

At the intersection of SH 420 and SH 10, the MRT turns right. You can turn left at this intersection for an optional side trip to historic St. Francisville. The route includes a ferry ride across the MR. This route is popular with tourists, so to beat the crowds, try arriving at the ferry in early morning or late afternoon. The ferry runs from 4:30 a.m. to 11:45 p.m.

In the town of New Roads, the turn onto SH 1 can be a little confusing, because there are two right turns for SH 1. The first right turn is for north SH 1. The MRT follows the second right turn. Once you know not to take the first SH 1 turn, the route is simple. Continue past the turn until the road dead-ends at the banks of the False River, and then turn right onto SH 1 south. At this point you are riding alongside the False River through downtown New Roads. It is a picturesque town with gift shops, eating places, coffee shops, motels, and anything else you might need. New Roads is the home to the Parlange Plantation House. Built in 1750, this is one of the oldest antebellum homes in Louisiana. Tours are available by appointment, by calling 225-492-2110. If you would like an extended plantation experience, you can spend a night at the White Hall Plantation House, a fully restored 1849 Greek revival home.

When you reach the town of Livonia, if you are in dire need of a bike shop, you can take a left on US 190 for a 30-mile side trip to Baton Rouge. I have included several of the city's bike shops for anyone desperate enough to make the ride. Maybe you can even call them to have them bring you whatever parts you need. As an FYI on the future of the MRT, there are plans in the works for building a 100-mile paved levee bike path linking the cities of Baton Rouge and New Orleans. I can't wait!

Camping

*River View RV Park
100 River View Parkway
Vidalia, LA
866-336-1402

*Deer Park Lake CG
144 Deer Park Rd
Vidalia, LA
318-336-7443

*Maxicare RV Park
641 Hwy 1
Morganza. LA
225-694-3929

Jim's Camping Area
7913 Park St
New Roads, LA
225-638-6286

Lodging

*Comfort Suites
100 Front St
Vidalia, LA
800-260-2715

*Sunrise on the River B&B
1825 False River Dr
New Roads, LA
225-638-3642

White Hall Plantation House
17523 Highway 418
New Roads, LA
225-492-2110

*Point Breeze Motel
2111 False River Dr
New Roads, LA
225-638-3414

Bike Shops

The Bicycle Shop
3315 Highland Rd
Baton Rouge, LA
225-344-5624

Dave's Bicycle Repair
Baton Rouge, LA
225-924-4337
(offers mobile service)

Capital Cyclery & Fitness
5778 Essen Lane
Baton Rouge, LA
225-766-4004

Pedal Play
13726 Perkins Rd
Baton Rouge, LA
225-761-9286

Vidalia to Livonia (104 miles)

Miles N/S	Directions	Dist	S	T	Services	Miles S/N
0	Enter LA on US 65 bridge	0.6	0	X		104
	*Vidalia				GLQR	
1	L onto SH 131/Martin Luther King Jr Ave	6.2	4	M	C	103
7	S onto SH 15	46.7	4	M	C	97
	*Deer Park Lake CG				C	
	*Primitive Camping				C	
54	L onto SH 418	9	1	L		50
63	L at SS onto SH 1 (*Innis)	2.8	8	H	GQ	41
65	L onto SH 419 (*Batchelor)	3.2	1	M	QR	38
69	R onto SH 972	2.3	0	M		35
71	L at SS onto SH 1	9.2	3	H	CGQR	33
	*Morganza				CGQR	
80	L onto SH 420	7.2	3	L		24
87	R onto SH 10 (SH 10 runs straight into SH 1. Do not take SH 1 North entering New Roads)	3	3	M	GQR	17
90	R at SL onto SH 1 (*New Roads)	6	0	H	CGLQR	14
96	R at SL onto SH 78	7.5	0	M	GQ	8
104	R at SL onto US 190					0
	*Livonia					

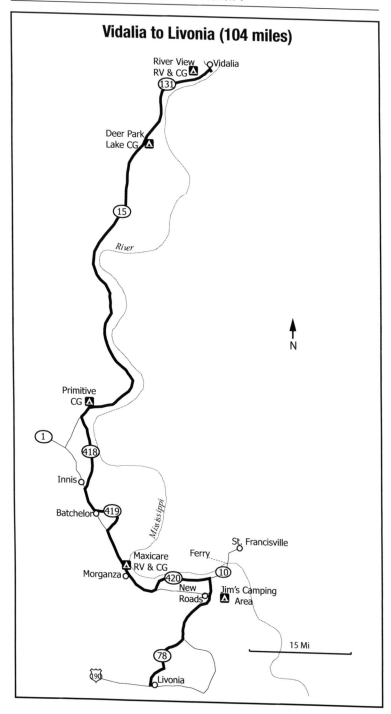

Vidalia to Livonia (104 miles)

River View RV & CG — Vidalia

(131)

Deer Park Lake CG

(15)

River

Primitive CG

(1)

(418)

Innis

Batchelor — (419)

Mississippi

Maxicare RV & CG

Morganza

(420)

St. Francisville

Ferry

(10)

New Roads

Jim's Camping Area

(78)

(190) — Livonia

N

15 Mi

Louisiana: Section 2
Livonia to Edgard (108 miles)

The route gets a little tricky in the town of Maringouin, as SH 977 rejoins SH 77. There is a flashing red light at the intersection where SH 77 comes in from the right and SH 977 continues to the left. The MRT continues straight across the intersection on SH 77 south, also called Grosse Tete Bayou Road. This road is named after the bayou the road parallels.

After rolling alongside the bayou for several miles, you need to watch for the metal grid on the bridge as SH 77 veers left to cross Port Allen Canal. The convenience store, located just across the bridge, is a good place to stop for a cool drink and a snack. About a mile after you cross the canal, watch for the 3066 spur bridge over the Intracoastal Waterway. The waterway borders the MRT as it enters the historic town of Plaquemine.

In Plaquemine, the MRT routes cyclists past a variety of places to eat. City Café and Cajun Country Café are both local favorites. Plaquemine is a good place to park your bike and stretch your legs on a walking tour. I recommend that you turn left on Main Street, and ride to the Plaquemine Lock State Historic Site to begin your tour. Within walking distance from this historic site, you can visit the Iberville Museum, John the Evangelist Catholic Church, St. Basil's Academy, and many other historic structures. If you are looking for a unique adventure, contact The Last Wilderness—225-659-2499—for a tour of the Atchafalaya Swamp.

There are several interesting attractions to visit along the next stretch of the MRT. The route passes Madonna Chapel, the smallest chapel in the world. There is an annual mass held at the chapel on August 15, to celebrate the Assumption of the Blessed Mother. The chapel is open daily, but if the door is locked, you can find the key in the mailbox. The MRT also passes the Nottoway Plantation, the largest antebellum plantation still in existence. The plantation offers tours, serves lunch and dinner, and is also a bed-and-breakfast.

In Donaldsonville, the MRT routes you through the historic section, and away from the commercial area. If you are in need of supplies, you can bypass the turn for SH 18 and continue straight on Albert Street, to reach a grocery store and restaurant. You can rejoin the MRT by following a side street in the direction of the river, or you can backtrack to SH 18.

Although SH 18 has medium-rated traffic, and no shoulder, it is an interesting ride. The highway is bordered on the riverside by a tall grass-covered levee, and on the other side by large homes, with huge live oaks on their front lawns. Many of the massive branches on these trees are as large as their trunks. I can imagine generations of children who have spent many summer hours playing on swings hanging from these branches. SH 18 will take you past what I consider to be the most impressive plantation home on the entire ride. Oak Alley Plantation has been called the "Grande Dame of the Great River Road." The home itself is not what sets it apart from the other beautiful homes. It is the quarter-mile canopy of 28 live oak trees lining the front entrance that makes it special. If you tour only one plantation on your trip, I suggest this one. It has a restaurant and operates a bed-and-breakfast in the cottages located on the plantation.

Three miles south of Oak Alley Plantation, the MRT passes one of my favorite seafood restaurants, B&C Seafood. This is a combination seafood market and restaurant, so you know the seafood is fresh. Their menu includes unique dishes, such as Alligator Sauce Piquante, Crawfish Stew, and Turtle Sauce Piquante. They also have a seafood platter that will satisfy even the hungriest cyclist. If you visit them on a Friday night, you can enjoy their "all you can eat" seafood buffet! If it is time to eat when you pass the restaurant, this is definitely a RS.

When you reach the community of Edgard, you get to take a ferry across the MR to the town of Reserve. The ferry operates weekdays from 5:15 a.m. until 8:45 p.m. and is closed on the weekends. If you arrive when the ferry is closed, you can backtrack 8 miles to the Veterans Memorial Bridge, located in Wallace. This bridge has a pretty good shoulder, but use caution. If you take the bridge, you can follow SH 44 south, to rejoin the MRT in Reserve.

I was unable to locate a campground for this section, so I guess you'll just have to tough it out and stay in a motel, or maybe even a plantation bed-and-breakfast.

Camping

N/A

Lodging

Oak Tree Inn
7875 Airline Highway
Livonia, LA
225-637-2590

Best Western Plantation Inn
2179 Highway 70
Donaldsonville, LA
225-746-9050

Best Western Plaquemine Inn
23235 Highway 1
Plaquemine, LA
225-385-4388

*Magnolia Motel
701 W 10th (Hwy 1)
Donaldsonville, LA
225-473-3146

*Nottoway Plantation (B&B)
30970 Highway 405
White Castle, LA
866-527-6884

*Oak Alley Plantation (B&B)
3645 Highway 18
Vacherie, LA
800-442-5539

Bike Shops

N/A

Livonia to Edgard (108 miles)

Miles N/S	Directions	Dist	S	T	Services	Miles S/N
	*Livonia					
0	R at SL onto US 190	0.1	0	M	GQR	108
0	L at SL onto SH 77	1	0	M		107
1	L onto SH 977	4.7	0	M		106
6	S onto SH 77 (*Maringouin)	23.4	0	M	GQR	102
	*Rosedale					
29	R onto 3066-spur (Bayou Rd)	0.1	0	M		78
29	L onto 3066-spur (Bayou Rd)	6.6	0	M		78
36	R at SL onto SH 1 (*Plaquemine)	0.7	0	M	QR	72
37	L onto SH 75/Belleview Rd	0.2	0	M	G	71
37	Curve R onto River Rd/ SH 405	29	0	M		71
	*White Castle				QR	
66	L at SS onto SH 1	3.3	8	M	L	42
69	L at SL onto SH 18 (*Donaldsonville)	38.4	0	M	GLQR	38
	*Vacherie				R	
108	*Edgard/Reserve Ferry					0

185

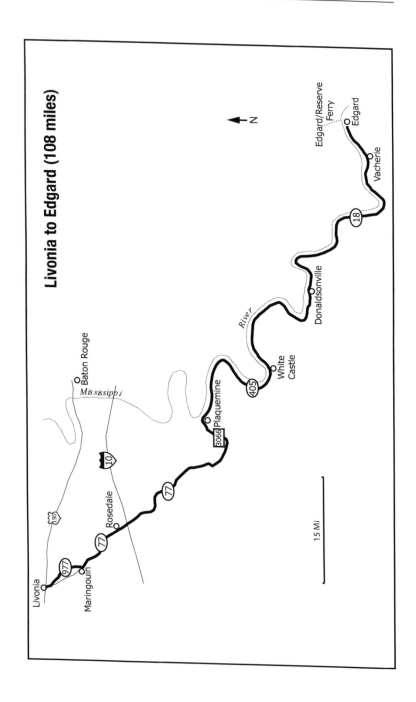

Livonia to Edgard (108 miles)

Louisiana: Section 3
Edgard to St. Bernard State Park (63 miles)

When you reach the east side of the MR by way of the Edgard-Reserve ferry, you will be riding on some very busy roads with little or no shoulder. As you should do with all major cities, try to schedule your approach into New Orleans during off-traffic hours. You have about 18 miles to ride before you reach the Levee Trail, so be patient and use caution. If you have wide tires you might consider riding the gravel levee whenever possible; just be sure to keep the MRT route in sight.

As you ride through the town of Montz, watch for the St. Charles Parish water tower. The tower is about a mile before the turnoff onto Spillway Road. This turn is easy to miss because there is no road sign for Spillway Road. I missed the turn the first time I rode through here. There may be a road sign or a MRT sign here in the future, but for now there is no sign. As River Road curves left and becomes Ccc Road, Spillway Road veers off to the right over the levee. There is a road sign at the turn for Ccc Road.

Spillway Road is an oasis in a sea of busy traffic. Once you are over the levee, you ride across a flat, wide drainage area, with little or no traffic. I don't know why they built a paved road in a spillway, but you'll be glad they did. As you reach the other side of the spillway, the road runs up the levee and curves right for less than $1/_{10}$ mile, then turns left, taking you back to River Road. It may seem a little confusing through here, but if you just stay on the paved road you won't get lost, because all other possible routes through here are either dirt or gravel.

You pass a few restaurants, several grocery stores, and some colorful local taverns along this stretch. You do have about a 1-foot shoulder now, but the traffic can be busy. About 6 miles after leaving Spillway Road, you reach the stop light for Ormond Boulevard. At the stop light, take the bike ramp off to the right to begin enjoying one of the true jewels of the MRT. The Levee Trail includes 22 miles of paved bike trail along the top of the levee, and 2 miles of paved trail through Audubon Park.. Cycling doesn't get any better than this. The Levee Trail is a memorial to Bill Keller, the former chairman of the New Orleans Regional Bicycle Awareness Committee.

Even though the Mileage Log has services listed for the Levee Trail, these businesses are actually on roads that parallel the trail.

A lot of the businesses are visible from the trail, such as the KOA, which is located about 11 miles into the trail. The campground is on Jefferson Highway, but you can see the sign from the Levee Trail. To reach the campground, watch for the street sign for Cumberland Street or Wilker Neal Avenue, and then push your bike down the side of the levee. For those who plan to camp at the KOA, if you reach the yield sign on the Levee Trail as it crosses the turn onto Florida Street, you have missed the turnoff to the KOA.

If you are in need of a bike shop, the closest one to the Levee Trail is Bicycle World of Louisiana. To reach the shop, you will exit the trail after about 19 miles. Look for the Iris Avenue street sign and follow it to Jefferson Highway, and then take a right.

The scenery from atop the levee is diverse, with views into the backyards of nice homes with swimming pools, to views of small houses on the river with vegetable gardens, and goats, and chickens. The view across the MR from on top of the levee is unmatched. Take a break on one of the benches to watch huge ships regally cruising past. You can daydream about stowing away on one of these ships and imagine where it might take you.

The Levee Trail ends in Audubon Park. Follow the park road across Magazine Street and into the park's main area. This beautiful park has a lake in the middle and is bordered by large antebellum homes. Go ahead and ride the loop around the lake, and when you are ready to leave, you will exit past a pair of large Greek columns onto St. Charles Avenue.

The Mileage Log follows a designated main route through New Orleans, but you don't want to limit your tour to a single route. If you pass an interesting neighborhood, take a detour. There are plans for marking alternate routes, but I encourage you to create your own. You can't go wrong. There are so many interesting sights to see and adventures to experience in New Orleans, no tour map can begin to cover them all. The main MRT route pretty much follows a consistent direction through town, so if you veer off to the right, just follow a leftward heading to return to the MRT.

The French Quarter should definitely be a RS on every cyclist's agenda. But where do you start in an area like this that offers so many attractions? By now you know the answer to this—the visitor center. The Jean Lafitte National Historical Park and Preserve French Quarter Visitor Center is conveniently located in the heart of the French Quarter at 419 Decatur Street. To reach the center, at the intersection of Camp and Julia streets, rather than turning left onto Julia Street, turn right. After a block on Julia Street, take a left onto Magazine Street, and this will run straight into Decatur Street. The center has films and exhibits that tell the unique history of the New Orleans area. I recommend that you take the park ranger lead walking tour. The area comes to life, as you hear the history and background of the French Quarter, and as you walk past the buildings with their wrought iron balconies, tall shutters and lush courtyards. When you are ready to leave the French Quarter, turn off of Decatur Street onto Toulouse Street, or Dumaine Street. Six blocks after leaving Decatur Street, you will cross North Rampart Street. When you turn right, you will once again be back on the route described in the Mileage Log.

Be sure to arrive at the French Quarter hungry. The food is a main part of the French Quarter experience. Cajun, French, or Creole, you can take your pick. Be sure to leave room for dessert, and top off your adventure with coffee and beignets on the patio at Café du Monde.

My wife, and my ride home, enjoying beignets at Café du Monde.

As you follow North Rampart Street, you may not even notice that it becomes McShane Place, a block before reaching St. Claude Avenue. The road just kind of curves around and you're on St. Claude Avenue. So don't get stressed out looking for McShane Place. I include McShane Place in the log mainly for the south-to-north cyclists. Once you are on St. Claude Avenue, you will cross a bridge with a metal grid surface. Use caution; these waffle grids can be dangerous.

If you are staying the night in New Orleans, there are plenty of motels and hotels to choose from. I have included a few that are located in the French Quarter, in case you want to call ahead for reservations. Believe it or not, New Orleans is set up really great for cyclists who are camping. You can camp at the KOA as you come into town, and then get an early start the next morning, and spend the day exploring the city. When you are ready to leave "the Crescent City," it's only an 18-mile ride out of town to St. Bernard State Park. Don't you just love it when things work out!

Camping

*KOA Campground
11129 Jefferson Hwy
New Orleans, LA
504-467-1792

*St. Bernard State Park
501 St. Bernard Parkway
Braithwaite, LA
504-682-2101

Lodging

Dauphine Orleans
415 Dauphine St
New Orleans, LA
800-521-7111

Holiday Inn Express
221 Carondelet St
New Orleans, LA
866-849-3484

Maison Dupuy
1001 Toulouse St
New Orleans, LA
800-535-9177

French Market Inn
501 Rue Decatur
New Orleans, LA
888-538-5651

Bike Shops

*Bicycle World of Louisiana
701 Jefferson Hwy
Jefferson, LA
504-828-1862

Bicycle Michael's LLC
622 Frenchman St
New Orleans, LA
504-945-9505

GNO Cyclery
1426 S Carrollton Ave
New Orleans, LA
504-861-0023

Eastbank Cyclery
1908 W Esplanade Ave
Kenner, LA
504-464-8803

Edgard to St. Bernard State Park (63 miles)

Miles N/S	Directions	Dist	S	T	Services	Miles S/N
	*Edgard					
0	R on SH 44/E Jefferson Hwy/W 5th St	4	0	H		63
4	S on SH 628	3.1	0	H		59
7	S on River Rd	3.5	0	H	Q	56
11	Veer R to go over levee onto Spillway Rd	1.5	0	L		52
12	S onto River Rd (after crossing the spillway)	6.6	1	X	QR	51
19	R at SL on The Levee Trail/Audubon Pk	23.9	P		CLQR	44
	*New Orleans				GLQR	
43	R on St Charles Ave	2.1	0	X	QR	20
45	R on Toledano St	0.1	0	X		18
45	L on Prytania	1.5	0	X		18
46	R on Clio St	0.1	0	X		17
46	L on Camp St	0.3	0	X		17
47	L on Julia St	0.3	0	X		16
47	R on O'Keefe Ave	0.5	0	X		16
48	L on Common St	0.1	0	X		16
48	R on S. Rampart St/N. Rampart St	1.1	0	X		15
49	S on McShane Pl	0.1	0	M		14
49	S on St Claude Ave	3.7	0	M		14
53	L on St Bernard Hwy	9.9	4	H	QR	11
62	R on St Bernard Pkwy	0.6	4	M	CG	1
63	*St. Bernard SP				C	0

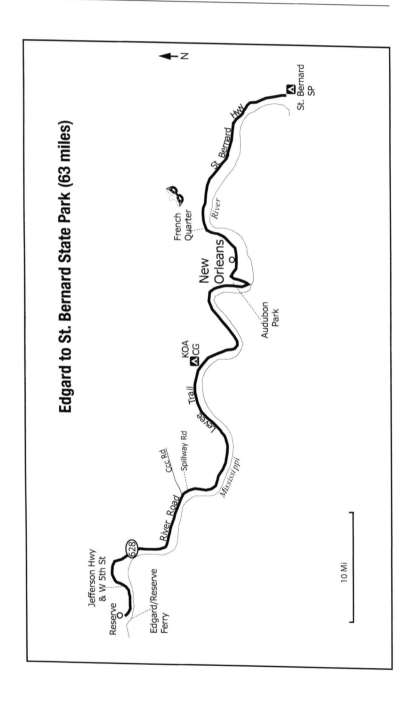

Edgard to St. Bernard State Park (63 miles)

Louisiana: Section 4
St. Bernard State Park to the Gulf of Mexico (75 miles)

Shortly after leaving St. Bernard State Park, you turn onto English Turn Road. While I was visiting the state park, I discovered the interesting origin of this road's name. In 1699, French navy commander Jean Baptiste Bienville encountered a company of Englishmen who were sailing up the MR to establish a British settlement. Bienville "convinced" Captain Lewis Banks that the territory was a possession of France, and the British commander turned around and left the area. The name has continued for over 300 years.

As you ride along this stretch, you get a true sense of the enormous size of the ships that use the MR. Even though the levee partially blocks your view, you can still see these tall vessels towering above the levee. It's hard to imagine the amount of cargo these huge ships can hold.

You pass more plantation homes on this route, and once you pick up a shoulder on SH 39, it becomes an even more relaxing ride. The route offers views of bayous filled with cranes, snowy egrets, and other waterfowl. Cyclists equipped for riding on a gravel road have the option of riding on top of the levee along this stretch. The MRT reaches the town of Pointe a la Hache, where you cross the MR on the Pointe a la Hache Ferry. The ferry operates on the half-hour, seven days a week, between 5:30 a.m. and 10:30 p.m. As you lean against the railing, during the ferry ride across this wide expanse of the MR, pause a moment to reflect back to the small stream you waded across at the beginning of the ride at Itasca State Park. It is difficult to associate the two images. If the MR were a living person, you would have watched it develop from a child to an adult in the course of your ride.

After you leave the ferry, point your bike south to begin the final leg of your MRT ride. This is a pretty enjoyable stretch of road to finish on. With an 8-foot shoulder, you can leisurely pedal these remaining miles as you reflect on your journey and all of your adventures. There are convenience stores and grocery stores along the route that provide stops for drinks and snacks. There are several RV parks on this stretch, but at this time none of them have restroom facilities for non-self-contained camping. The owner of Yellow Cotton Bayside Cabin Rentals and RV Park did tell me that he has plans to install facilities to accommodate camping for cyclists.

I have added the contact information so you can check the status of the campground when you plan your trip. There are several motels along the route. For those considering a return to New Orleans via SH 23, rather than taking the Pointe a La Hache ferry back, be aware that north of the ferry crossing, SH 23 becomes very busy and is not as bike-friendly as SH 39 across the river.

You are now riding on a peninsula at this point. Many of the businesses you pass in the small towns along this stretch are associated with the charter-fishing industry. These charter boats benefit by having the MR run through the middle of the peninsula. Unlike charter fishermen on the coast, who have to venture great distances across the open Gulf waters to reach deep-water fishing environments, the MR provides fishermen with a safe route to the deep offshore waters. From the mouth of the MR, they only have to travel a short 10 miles across the open Gulf waters before the bottom plummets to 100 feet.

As it leaves Venice, the route takes you past an industrial area. Continue to follow the paved highway through here, veering right at all intersections. When I rode this final leg of the route, I thought that after all of the beautiful scenery I had ridden through, surely the MRT wasn't going to end at the gates of a petroleum plant. Shortly after this, I rode across a spit of land that routed me away from the industrial area. The patch of land wasn't much wider than the pavement of the road, with water bordering both sides. Water had even washed across the road in some places. I startled a pelican that was feeding in the marsh beside the road, and as it struggled to gain flight, this magnificent bird paralleled my route alongside the highway. For 20 feet we traveled in unison. I smiled and nodded to the beautiful bird as it flew at eye level, thanking it for making the finish of my ride such a memorable one.

It may not be the most scenic finish for a cross-country bike ride, but when you reach the sign stating that you have reached the southernmost point in Louisiana, I'm sure it will be a beautiful sight for you.

CONGRATULATIONS!!!!

THE END OF THE ROAD!

Camping

*St. Bernard State Park
501 St. Bernard Parkway
Braithwaite, LA
504-682-2101

Yellow Cotton Bayside Cabins
& RV Park
40702 Hwy 23
Boothville, LA
504-534-2570

Lodging

Woodland Plantation B&B
21997 Highway 23 (2 miles
north of ferry)
West Point a la Hache, LA
800-231-1514

Venice Inn Motel
42660 Highway 23
Venice, LA
504-534-7424

*Empire Inn
32022 Highway 23
Buras, LA
504-657-9853

*Lighthouse Lodge
42256 Highway 23
Venice, LA
504-534-2522

Bike Shops

N/A

St. Bernard State Park to the Gulf of Mexico (75 miles)

Miles N/S	Directions	Dist	S	T	Services	Miles S/N
	*St. Bernard SP				C	
0	S on St Bernard Pkwy	0.4	4	M		75
0	S on SH 39	2.4	3	M		75
3	R onto English Turn Rd/CR 3137	3.8	0	M		72
7	S on SH 39	25.9	3	M	Q	68
33	R onto Adema Ln	0.4	0	M		42
33	L onto SH 15	0.2	0	M		42
33	R to Pointe a la Hache Ferry					42
	*Ferry across the MR	0.3				
33	L at SS onto SH 23	38.1	8	M	GLQR	42
	*Port Sulphur				GQR	
	*Buras				LQR	
	*Boothville				CL	
	*Venice				GLQR	
72	R at SS onto Tidewater Rd (no sign)	3.4				3
75	Sign indicating the southernmost point in Louisana					0
	The End of the MRT					

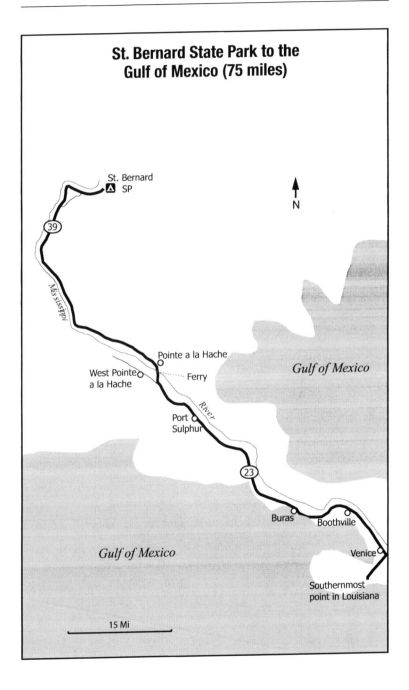

St. Bernard State Park to the Gulf of Mexico (75 miles)

N

St. Bernard SP

39

Mississippi

Pointe a la Hache

West Pointe a la Hache ···· Ferry

Gulf of Mexico

Port Sulphur

River

23

Buras

Boothville

Gulf of Mexico

Venice

Southernmost point in Louisiana

15 Mi

INDEX

About the Author

Bob Robinson has been an avid cyclist for over 25 years. During this period he has raced both road and mountain bikes, organized races for both road and mountain bikes, built mountain bike trails, served as cycling club president, organized bicycle tours, and worked as a committee member for the National Trails Symposium. Bob strongly believes in actively supporting sports that he participates in.

The author with a friend he met in Red Wing, Minnesota.

Bob and his wife, Dawna, are avid backpackers. They recently fulfilled a goal of backpacking the Chilkoot Pass Trail, outside of Skagway, Alaska. They also have visited all of the 50 states in our beautiful country. The couple live in Fort Smith, Arkansas, within a short drive to the Ozark Mountains and the Ouachita Mountains. They are both active members of the Ozark Highlands Trail Association and the Friends of the Ouachita Trail organization.

Bob looks forward to meeting cyclists, and sharing stories with them around the campfire, during his future rides along the Mississippi River Trail, as he researches updates to the guidebook.

Made in the USA